# HUMAN BEING AS A TRIPARTITE; BODY, SOUL AND SPIRIT

Understand Why Your Body is a
Battleground Between Good and Evil

DAVID D. WEL

*A Note from the Publisher*

The publisher wishes to acknowledge and thank Dr Douglas H. Johnson for his invaluable help and support for Africa World Books and its mission of preserving and promoting African cultural and literary traditions and history. Dr Johnson and fellow historians have been instrumental in ensuring that African people remain connected to their past and their identity. Africa World Books is proud to carry on this mission.

© David D. Wel, 2021

ISBN: 978-0-6452105-6-9

All rights reserved

No part of this publication may be reproduced, stored in a retrieval system, or transmitted, in any form, or by any means, electronic, mechanical, photocopying, recording or otherwise, without the prior permission of the publishers.

This book is sold subject to the conditions that it shall not, by way of trade or otherwise, be lent, re-sold, hired out or otherwise circulated without the publisher's prior consent in any form of binding or cover other than in which it is published and without a similar condition including the condition being imposed on the subsequent purchaser.

Cover design, typesetting and layout: Africa World Books
Cover image: freepik/nikitabuida

# DEDICATION

This book is dedicated to my wonderful family, who had and have always supported everything I do.

To my father, late Wel Deng Ayom; Mothers, Late Akuol Chol Khang and Nyang Akec Akur, who took care of me in my early childhood years. I am who I am today because of my late father Who at, young age imparted into me the values of courage, determination, passion, and commitment to the cause of my life.

To my siblings, Yar Wel Deng, Alier Wel Deng, Kuany Wel Deng, Madol Wel Deng, Akon Wel Deng, Late Ayen Wel Deng, Ateng Wel Deng, Abiei Wel Deng, Late Majak Wel Deng, Kuol Wel Deng, Ayor Wel Deng and Deng Wel Deng, for their continuous Love, support, and encouragement to me. Particularly to my brother Kuol Wel Deng, who was instrumental in guiding and directing my life at young age in the areas of education and other social welfare.

To all my beloved nephews and nieces just to mention few; Alier Kuol Wel, Ding Abiei Wel and Kuany Yar Wel, who have given me their words of encouragement in writing the books and of course to Late nephew Ayom Majak Wel, who was always there for me in support all of my endeavours.

I am also indebted to the African World Books Publishers and Particularly Peter Lual Reec Deng, for his determination and commitment in the designing, printing, and the distribution of the books across the world. Your commitment to see that the books receive international coverage and outreach will never go unnoticed forever in my life. Without a doubt it has been a work of God to team up with you. May the living God continue to bless the work of your hands.

# TABLE OF CONTENTS

| | |
|---|---|
| Acknowledgments | vii |
| Prologue | ix |
| Introduction | xv |

**Part I: The Human Body** — 1

Chapter 1: The Human Body is Wonderfully Made by God — 5

Chapter 2: The Body as a Temple of The Holy Spirit — 14

Chapter 3: The Body as a Mechanism of Work — 29

Chapter 4: Body as The Healthy You — 38

Chapter 5: The Body as a Battleground Between Good and Evil, to Each Carry Out Their Agenda — 54

Chapter 6: Body if Saved Will be Reunited With Your Spirit and Soul After The Coming of Christ — 67

**Part II: Soul, The Engine of Human Operation** — 73

Chapter 7: Will (Desires) — 79

Chapter 8: Mind (Thoughts and Imaginations) — 94

Chapter 9: Emotions (Moods and Attitudes) — 111

Chapter 10: Our Soul if Saved Will Go to Heaven and if Not Saved, to Hell When We Die — 124

**Part III: Spirit** 134
Chapter 11: Spirit Created in The Image of God 139
Chapter 12: Spirit as a Receiving Aerial From God 147
Chapter 13: The Spirit as a Sending Aerial to God 157
Chapter 14: Spirit if Saved Will Go Back to God 172

Bibliography 179
About The Author 181

# ACKNOWLEDGEMENTS

Let me thank the people who have individually written to me, encouraging me with their private messages about the goodness of the DW Spiritual Care International online discussion program on impacting people's lives. To those people who had thrown their likes, comments, and questions for improvement in the support of our online program and the writing of the books, I say thank you. To those people who were a little bit uncomfortable with the program with few concerns here and there that had pushed me to do more, I am also thankful to you. For without you the critics, I wouldn't have known what I am doing wrong. I am indebted and humbled by you all, for you are the reason why I am doing what I am doing. Special thank you to those who have bought for themselves the copies of the books and who have also come back, with the positive feedbacks of the greatness and impacts, the books have to their lives.

    I will leave it to you the followers and the supporters of our program, to judge whether the program has really impacted your lives and thinking about the word of God in positive or negative ways. My job is to and will continue to be about bringing the word of God closer to you, individually, including writing more books. No one can be your best friend in this dangerous world than the God of heaven. No one in this dangerous world will look after you, protect you and supply all your needs than the God of heaven. Make him your friend and you will be deeply rooted and grounded in him. The only stumbling block between you and him is your unbelieve. He is in the supernatural, and you are in the natural, and he wants you to access him by faith. That is all that is required of you. Without Faith you cannot please him.

To My dear wife Rachel Awuok Ayuel, you have been the great force behind everything I do including writing this book. Although we continue to face challenges on the most important aspects of our lives, that makes a complete family, you continue to defy all odds to stick by me. Even today when the forces of darkness are trying to break us apart, I am sure we will overcome them. Because nothing breaks the zeal of people who have a united vision and mission in life. You promised me a little under ten (10) years ago, when you gave your hand in marriage to me, to stick by me whether in good or bad times. The case which I was not sure by then that we will fall into a big one, which continues to foreshadow and threatens our togetherness today. You have done more for me than a husband should have ask or expect from a wife. Thank you so much for that.

Special thank you to Dr Ajak Duany Ajak and his wife Maggy Adol Aman for their unwavering commitment in support of DW Spiritual Care International programs. Dr Ajak has been instrumental to me in the works of structuring, editing, and proofreading of the books.

Finally let me thank my greatest master of the universe, the living God of heaven in the order of God almighty, God the son and God the holy spirit for their guidance for me in bringing the message to you on a weekly basis through our online discussion program for the last two years.

" The greatest tragedy is to be born into this world as a human being, live here, and leave it having not known the creator of it."

# PROLOGUE

This book will deal with this fundamental question of life; are you a body, body and soul or body, soul, and spirit? Unless you have answered this fundamental question correctly, life will have no meaning here on earth. This question had disturbed me for several years until it was settled and without a doubt, this question is also disturbing you and it will now be settled through this book. But not only your purpose here on earth, but your afterlife will also be dealt with at length and in great depth so that you can rediscover yourself before it is too late. Unless you understand and define yourself, life will have no meaning.

Have you ever asked yourself these questions; What is my life, what is my purpose and what will my life be afterlife on earth? You must answer these questions before you leave earth because life is real as you live, sleep, eat, breath, talk, dance, jump, work, move and you see other people around you and the entire universe you live in. People have wondered about the purpose of life for many centuries; philosophers have come up with theories in answering these questions of life, poets have written songs and poems about life, and scientists have attempted to answer these questions through many studies of both animals and plants that ended up associating us with apes. Very interesting indeed, these questions without a doubt will remain unanswered by many people unless they consult the book of life – the bible, which talks about the creation of humans, their purpose, and their afterlife.

The origin and the creation of the world we live in today is so complex and confusing because of the conflicting opinions of its origin given to us by men and women who think they are experts on the history of creation. The two lenses through which we see, read, and get informed about the origin of the world and its creation history today are Religion and science. Depending on the available information to individuals from these two sources, people could conclusively take either of two histories of the creation origin by supporting the religion or the science version. Why is this happening now? Because the current scientists no longer acknowledge God as the sole creator of the universe, as did previous scientists. Many of them have rejected the existence of God, let alone his creation of the universe. They have refused to believe the history of creation in the bible and decided to venture out with their own history of creation that is totally different from the bible and which does not acknowledge God or attribute the beautiful work of creation to him. Even as they are denying God as the creator of the universe, they have not given us, or come up with a new creator of the universe. So, they are giving their version of creation without giving credit to the creator. What you will hear from most of the scientists today is that the world came to existence from nothing – hence no one should be given the credit for its origin. To that effect, they have instead come up with theories such as evolution theory, purporting that mankind came from the apes or the monkeys if you like. As a result, people are confused today due to this alternative competitive history of creation over that one of the bible. Not only are humans being confused over the history of creation, but their identity has also been confused.

Today people are confused on how to answer this question; Are we human beings originated from God or monkeys? Those who believe in science or religion will answer this question differently based on the information available to them and the version of creation they believe in. Very confusing indeed, but I have come to put this nonsense to rest using this book. God is the sole creator of the universe, and as a matter of fact, no scientists will challenge me on this. God created and science discovers through the work of scientists. This is how it should have been, and this is how it should be. Without brushing off completely the work of science I will acknowledge it here and there in this book, but I will predominantly use the bible to prove to you the work of God in creation, including the creation of mankind which the book is all about. Putting back the origin and the creation of mankind to his rightful owner, God, is the main reason why this book has been written. Although there is confusion about creation and the origin of the universe including the origin of mankind, science does not clearly explain the origin, purpose, and the final destiny of mankind after this life on earth, but the bible does. Not only does science fail to explain the origin, it does not acknowledge human beings as a triune – three in one – body, but the bible does.

For mankind to understand the whole history of the creation of God, we first need to understand ourselves, our origin, purpose, and destiny. This can only be done through the bible, which does acknowledge human beings as a triune – three in one body. According to the Bible, mankind is a spirit living in a body and with the soul. We cannot see the spirit part of us, but we can see the body and we can feel the soul and what is going on in it. In short, we are Spirit, soul, and body according to the bible. Here is the breakdown; Spirit (food is the word of God), Soul (food are wisdom and understanding), and body (food are natural plants and animal products). For each part of us mentioned, God has a plan. Hence, you can see how beautiful the work of God and the creation of mankind is. God has designed you and me in a way that all these three parts must depend on him while here on earth – on his mission. If you have voluntarily disconnected any of the three parts of you from him, then you have wilfully or un-wilfully joined the devil. This is not strange to understand, as today we have atheists and agnostics who denounce the existence of God, and who have believed in the work of their fellow human beings' creation – which is science. Let me make myself clear; anything that mankind considers outside God is an idol. An idol is considered by God as the worshipping of another god – Satan. As a matter of fact, there is no true spiritual growth in a person who denies the existence of God, and the devil who has just blind-folded them continues to beat them down and drive them into the dark world of science without God.

God has already determined our vision and mission here on earth – a purpose for every single human being which science cannot give us. It is only when you read the bible that you will exactly know what you were created for. That looks like good news to you, but the bad news is that you cannot achieve it without the help of God, because the devil knows it better than you do, and he is against it. Take note; all of us (mankind), came from heaven but not all of us(mankind), will go back to heaven. Let me justify this statement.

I have good news for you whether you are Christian or not, that there is a God who can give you full freedom here on earth to live your life free of bondage and with victory, in every single battle you will find on your way as you are travelling in the perfect will of God. The choice is yours either to believe that there is God, his son (Jesus Christ) and the holy spirit, who has a perfect plan for each one of you in this life and the life to come. The holy spirit living in you can give you his grace, ability, power, and the means to live a complete life and fulfil your divine destiny here on earth. The alternative is to choose not to believe in Jesus Christ, who came and died for you, for you to live a complete life here on earth, and you can continue to live your own life seeking after your ways, interests, and desires, when reject God and his plan for you.

So, it comes down to two things – you are either a fully surrendered Christian operating and working in God's perfect will, or you are a non-Christian who is carnal (fleshly), living your life without God, playing the cards of good luck and bad luck until you die. The living God of heaven and earth has made his divine life, opportunity, destiny, and power available to those believers who will truly seek him and live their lives in the complete will of God. This is the true born-again Christian; you are now a child of the highest God and you do not have to settle on mediocrity. Instead, you can enter God's best life for you which can start now where you are if you are truly hungry for things of God. Submit to him and find your complete freedom in him.

# INTRODUCTION

The biblical perspective must be the lens through which we should view the world and all the created things in it as Christians. All things on earth both living and non-living came to existence because of God's creation. This book puts back God at the centre stage of the creation of mankind. But not only that, mankind was created by God in three forms, body, soul and spirit, and all in one physical body. Among these beautiful creations by God, humans were uniquely created in his image to control and dominate God's other creations on earth. Humans were created as a triune with spirit, soul, and body that make them more powerful than other God creations. So, mankind is a spirit, soul (both created in God-image), and living in the body. What makes mankind unique among other God creations, is the human soul which gives the ability to control and dominate other creations. This subject of human beings –body, soul and spirit is a very controversial one, in which many people including even some religious leaders and biblical scholars are not in agreement if indeed human beings are triune. I consider this subject to be the basis on which the Christian faith should be established by all the people of faith, to fight the successful battle against the encroaching science community, that is trying to lead the world away from its source of creation. This brings me to the important fundamental questions of the study in this book: is the human being triune? Are we human beings really body and soul? or body, soul, and spirit? These questions cannot be perfectly answered unless we go straight into the word of God.

Let us start with the formation of the body from the book of Genesis 2:7- "***and the Lord God formed man of the dust of the ground…***" So, from this verse, God almighty formed mankind from the dust of the ground. This fact is scientifically proven that all elements of the human body come from the soil of the ground or dust of the earth. When one dies, the elements of the human body decompose and go back into the ground as dust. Please continue to pay attention as we move to the next part which is the soul.

Genesis 2:7- ***"and the Lord God formed man of the dust of the ground and breathed into his nostrils the breath of life, and man became a living being (soul)."*** It is important to note that in other translations of the bible, "living being," is also called "living Soul. "If you have confusion or if you cannot understand the word soul or being, then its original meaning in Hebrew is Nephesh. You can also look at that or research further the word to have a better understanding of it. That aside, let us go back to our topic, where we agreed that the man's body was formed out of dust on the ground. However, that was not enough for a human being to perform its functions, as his body lacked life. Watch this life had to come into him now in another process. In the second half of the same verse, Genesis 2:7, God had to do something else for mankind to have life; God breathed into his nostrils the breath of life, and the man became a living being (soul). So, God had to breathe into the nostrils of the man for him to have life. So, what is really the human Soul? And the answer is: a soul is what gives life to the body (dust of the ground) for a person to have life. Hence without a soul, the body is nothing or dust. For a person to think, speak and work he or she must have a soul and not only that, all living things have souls, but they do not have spirits. Let us go one step further; so, where exactly does the soul sit in the body?

Leviticus 17:11-14- *"'For the life of the flesh is in the blood, and I have given it to you upon the altar to make atonement for your souls; for it is the blood that makes atonement for the soul.' "Therefore, I said to the children of Israel, 'No one among you shall eat blood, nor shall any stranger who dwells among you eat blood.' "Whatever man of the children of Israel, or the strangers who dwell among you, who hunts and catches any animal or bird that may be eaten, he shall pour out its blood and cover it with dust; "for it is the life of all flesh. Its blood sustains its life. Therefore, I said to the children of Israel, 'You shall not eat the blood of any flesh, for the life of all flesh is its blood. Whoever eats it shall be cut off".* We have seen from the book of Genesis that what gives life to the body of humans is the soul, and here in the book of Leviticus we have also seen that the soul is the blood of mankind including all other living things that have blood. It is apparently clear now that what sustains human beings from generation to generation is the blood (soul), which is passed down from generation to generation. With this in mind, it is fair to say that from one man (Adam) our blood has sustained us and has been passed down from him to us today, and even to the generations who will come after us. It is the blood of every living thing that has sustained it and given it life. **Acts 17:26-** *"And He has made from one blood every nation of men to dwell on all the face of the earth and has determined their reappointed times and the boundaries of their dwellings."*

Up to this point, we have seen that mankind was formed out of the dust of the ground and given soul (blood) through the breath of God into the nostrils to have life. Not only human beings but all the living (animals) have souls and bodies created by God. So, we have seen here that God is the sole custodian of both the human body and soul. We must now agree that all mankind has both body (dust of the ground) and souls (blood which is the life of mankind). It can be concluded that Adam and Eve did not physically disappear from the earth when they had eaten the forbidden tree of knowledge of good and evil, but they lived on for several years after they had been cursed by God. We understand Adam lived to be 930 years on earth. Now we must agree that Adam and Eve did not lose their bodies and souls when they had eaten from the tree of knowledge of good and evil, but they lost something else. And if this is so then what had to die immediately, when he and she violated God's instructions not to eat from the tree of knowledge of God and evil? Please stay with me as we continue to go back to the bible.

Genesis 1:26-27- *"Then God said, "Let us make man in our image, according to Our likeness; let them have dominion over the fish of the sea, over the birds of the air, and over the cattle, over all the earth and over every creeping thing that creeps on the earth."* This is a mind-blowing scripture on what did die on that day when Adam and Eve ate from the tree of knowledge of good and evil. We understand here that God created mankind in his own image. So, Adam was created in the image of God. This begs the question, what is the image of God Adam was created from? We now agree it is not the body (dust of the ground) and Soul (blood which is the life of him).

John 4:24- *"God is Spirit, and those who worship Him must worship in spirit and truth."* This verse tells us that God is a spirit and so

Adam was made in the image of God the (Spirit). So, Adam was a spirit. To this effect, Adam in addition to his body and soul had the spirit in the image of God who is a spirit. If this does confuse you "in his image," then let us look at it in other verses of the bible. Genesis 5:1-5- ***"This is the book of the genealogy of Adam. In the day that God created man, He made him in the likeness of God. He created them male and female and blessed them and called them Mankind on the day they were created. And Adam lived one hundred and thirty years, and begot a son in his own likeness, after his image, and named him Seth. After he begot Seth, the days of Adam were eight hundred years; and he had sons and daughters. So, all the days that Adam lived were nine hundred and thirty years; and he died".*** These verses indicate that Adam fathered his children in his likeness or his image. What does this mean? So as Adam was, so were his children in his image, which was the image of God. As indicated by the bible God is not a body or a soul but a spirit. So, Adam was a spirit and so are the generations of his offspring including us today. So, God is a spirit, Adam is a spirit and so we are spirits (we human beings who are the descendants of Adam). Please let me take you a bit further; Why did God create Adam in His own image, as a spirit?

God created Adam in His own image for him (Adam) to communicate with him (God). We know that body and soul do not communicate with God because they are not like God. They are God's wonders and the greatness of his creation. For example, you cannot receive messages and images from the television outlets unless you have a television antenna or signal in your house. So, the antennae of both the body and soul is the Spirit which communicates with God. When it comes to things of God you need spirit to communicate while body and soul function through your five senses. The reason why we always fail to understand things of spirits as human beings is the fact that we attempt to understand them through our bodies and souls while neglecting our spirits. In conclusion, Adam was created out of the dust of the ground (Body); a soul which gave life to his body (which was his blood); and a spirit (in the image of God), for him to communicate with God. This is the true source of the creation of not only human beings but also all the living and nonliving things today on earth. Let no one attempt to discredit God's marvellous works and wonders of his creation. We can now look at what happened in the garden of Eden when mankind through Adam rebels. God had to withdraw his spirit from mankind. So, Adam and Eve had to live for several years after the withdrawal of God's spirit as bodies and souls, but without the spirits. With the withdrawal of God's spirit, mankind was cut off from communication with God until the spirit of God was restored to him during the day of Pentecost. So, let us look at the alternative lifestyle of mankind without the spirit of God.

Alternatively, there are other ways pointing to the origin of the universe and its creation which mankind must avoid. This view came because mankind were swayed away or were at odds with God, in the Garden of Eden. Because of mankind's rebellion against God, the world and its creation were cursed by God (Genesis 3). As a result of this curse, God had to cut off his relationships with mankind who were then left with the devil who had to poison their thinking about the origin of the universe and mankind. This alternative view of the world, origin and creation remains very controversial to date, as mankind continues to reject God even after he has reconciled himself to the world and humans through the death of his son-Jesus Christ on the cross. Because of that fall, at the garden of Eden the majority of humans today continues to distract or redirect many people away from God through literature and information that avoid God and his existence. A majority of people continue to dismiss and reject what happened at the garden of Eden, and instead, feed people of the world with wrong creation history and the origin of the universe. Due to their actions, the world today continues to have controversial views about the origin of the universe and its creation. They continue to dismiss the Bible account of the origin of mankind and the whole creation, either by being ignorant or being disobedient to the facts and the truth in the bible explaining the origin of all things including mankind. Through theories such as evolution, mankind is purported to have originated from apes. Through theories such as evolution, the big bang, and blackspot, the world is alleged to have originated from a small black spot out of the galaxy. The worst of all theories is the evolution theory that points or associates mankind with monkeys and asserts mankind originated from apes. There is nothing true about all these theories as they are aimed at distracting mankind from its true owner, who is God almighty. But this is all fatal as humans continue to be challenged by God through natural disasters, diseases, wars, and death, which are all hidden from humans and their wisdom.

To understand the universe God created correctly and use the data, information and knowledge obtained from scientific research appropriately and effectively, mankind must pursue science and technology according to the biblical world view. Science is mankind's way of observing, understanding, and explaining the origin and operation of the universe and its inhabitants. Technology is the use of the data, information and knowledge obtained through scientific research for the benefits of mankind and their better ways of controlling creation. It is only through the biblical worldview that a person can come to the true understanding of the origin, nature, purpose and behaviour of themselves and the universe they live in. That is why the book is pointing you back to your creator-God. It will be proven below, why it is fatal to be without God. There is no clarity of things without God and his wisdom. The only way we can understand things of God is to have the wisdom of God. You cannot have the wisdom of God until you accept God as your creator and more importantly accept his spirit to operate through you. It is only when we have the third part (Spirit), that we can understand the things of God. The only way we can communicate with God is to have the spirit of God communicating with our spirits.

When I speak about this, I know what I am talking about. Over years I attempted desperately to connect to God through prayers, fasting, reading the bible, and listening to many sermons by great men of God but all in vain. I was using my soul and body to try to connect to God but ignoring the third part of me – the spirit me. Why was this happening to me? Because I was not conscious of the fact that there was a third part of me – the spirit, which needed to be connected first before everything else. No one had talked to me about my spirit. Not many people including preachers talk about the spirit part of humans today in churches unless they are born-again Christians. This was not my problem alone but the problem of many people of the world today; they try to connect to God using their bodies and their souls but not their spirits. When we arrogantly try to connect to God or if you like, try to know things of God using our souls, we are using human wisdom. Human wisdom will never get us closer to God. Unless you acknowledge the third part of you – the spirit you, you will never know the things of God. I will bring to you the verses in the bible in support of this argument; Proverbs 4:20-23- *"My son, give attention to my words; incline your ear to my sayings. Do not let them depart from your eyes; keep them in the midst of your heart; for they are life to those who find them, and health to all their flesh. Keep your heart with all diligence, for out of it spring the issues of life".*

"Keep your heart with all diligence, for out of it spring the issues of life." The heart here in this verse means our spirits. God is trying to tell us here that we must guide our spirits with absolute care and special attention because that is where the information important for our lives comes from. In short, we must admit that God communicates with us through our spirits, not our bodies and our souls.

Shockingly as well, there are some people who are aware of their third part (spirit), yet never allow him to communicate with God. They do not admit the fact that their bodies are the temple of the spirit God, and the only place in their bodies where the spirit (holy spirit), sits and operates is through their spirits. If they are lucky to know then they quench the spirit of God by not being willing to listen and be obedient to him.

Furthermore, we must allow the spirit of God to run the show for us because he knows everything about us. It is only when we allow the spirit of God to operate through our spirit that we can know the things of God. It is the spirit of God who knows the will of God, and it is him who can reveal it to us. The only way we can have the full meaning of life and the real assignment for our lives, in this life now on earth is to allow the spirit of God to reveal it to us. The purpose for which we were created by God and sent to earth will only be revealed to us by the spirit of God. When we allow the spirit of God to work through us, he keeps us humble. It is out of God's humility that we can know the things of God. I will challenge the human wisdom below, to prove to you why you need God.

You must approach things of God, through the position of need not the position of satisfaction.

It is foolishness for mankind to be born into this world, with no idea of how it came into being, only to turn around later, after a few years of life in the world, and say, Oh I know how this world came about. It is also foolishness for people to leave this world having not known how it came about, only to be told by God that they are going to hell. Because you did not bother to find me while you had a chance to find me. Once you are dead, the responsibility as to where you will go does not rest with you. Pause about that a moment. Whether you oppose it or not, it does not change anything at all about heaven and hell. That is why the prophet Isaiah said, "**Seek the Lord while He may be found, call upon Him while He is near. Let the wicked forsake his way, and the unrighteous man his thoughts; Let him return to the Lord and He will have mercy on him; and to our God, for He will abundantly pardon.**"

God does not need your knowledge. It is of no help to him. He did not give knowledge to you to help him but rather, to help yourself and your fellow humans. He provides you with knowledge, abilities, and skills to understand the hard things of mankind to help your fellow humans. If you want to know things of God, you must shun human wisdom. You must approach things of God through the position of need not the position of satisfaction. No PhD, master's degree and Degree will enable you to know things of God. God hates the proud and He only teaches the humble. So, let no one boast in himself or others. If there were no challenges beyond human wisdom, mankind would not need God at all. Mankind does not like death, but it happens. Humans do not like wars, but they happen. Humans do not like diseases, but they catch them. Mankind does not like poverty, but they live with it. So, where is mankind's wisdom in solving all these things? The wisdom of humans comes to nothing if tough situations hit them such as sicknesses (cancer, HIV aids, Ebola); natural disasters (hurricanes, tsunamis, earthquake, volcanic eruptions, and storms); and all forms of accidents; planes, car, ships; and all forms of family difficulties, divorce, finances, and childlessness. You do not need to wait to be hit by one of the above disasters to know God. Before you become desperate and helpless in search of God, at difficult moments of need, now is the time.

God only shows up in the affairs of humans when their wisdom is completely exhausted and no more. You can be educated but still, live a miserable life if you are not with God. Here are the reasons why you need God throughout your life. He has held back his wisdom, courage, and understanding to be accessible only by those who wholeheartedly seek him in love. That is why you can have your education but remain helpless without his wisdom to apply what you have learned, daily over difficult matters of life. **Isaiah 55:8-12 says,** *"For My thoughts are not your thoughts, nor are your ways My ways," says the Lord. "For as the heavens are higher than the earth, so are My ways higher than your ways, and My thoughts than your thoughts. For as the rain comes down, and the snow from heaven, and do not return there, but water the earth, and make it bring forth and bud, that it may give seed to the sower and bread to the eater, so shall My word be that goes forth from My mouth; it shall not return to Me void, but it shall accomplish what I please, and it shall prosper in the thing for which I sent it. "For you shall go out with joy and be led out with peace; the mountains and the hills shall break forth into singing before you, and all the trees of the field shall clap their hands."*

The mysteries of God kingdom simply beat mankind's logic and wisdom. If what you see is what you believe, then you will miss God. God is a spirit – you can never see him. Now is the time for you to launch into the spirit world through this book.

# HUMAN BEING AS TRIPARTITE; BODY, SOUL & SPIRIT

## *THE MANIFESTATION OF A PERSON WHO CONTINUES TO LIVE BY FLESH AND NOT BY THE SPIRIT*

### LIVING ACCORDING TO THE FLESH
1 Corinthians 3:3 carnal 'Christians' behaving like mere men; 3:16 "Do you not know that you are the temple of God and that the Spirit of God dwells in you?"

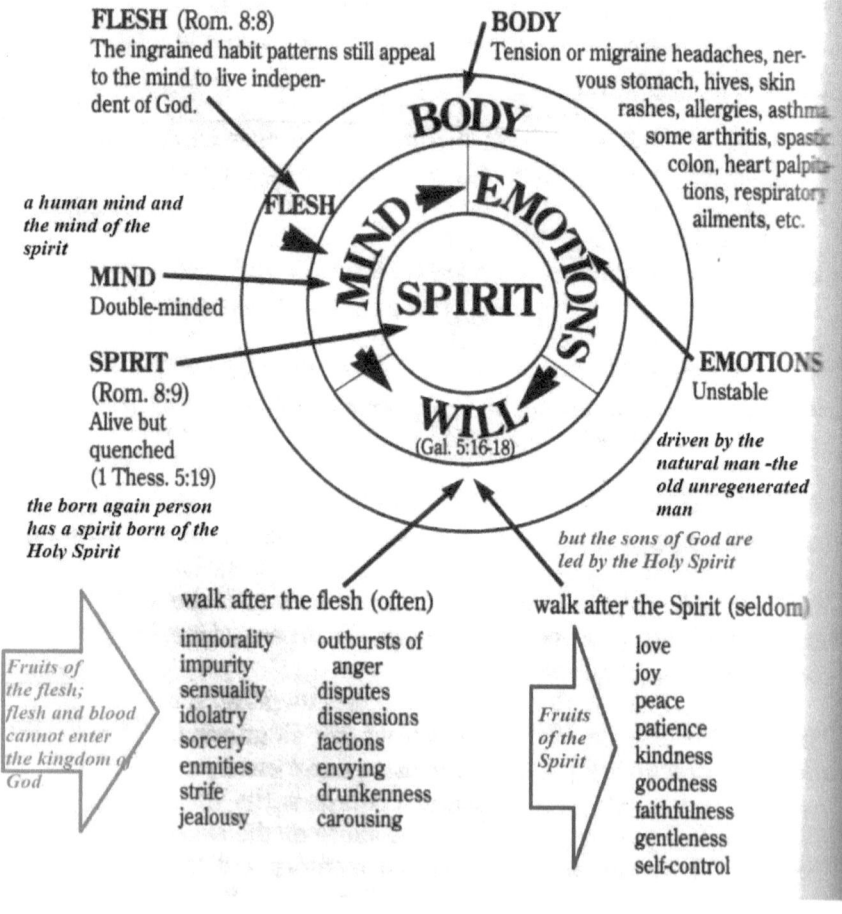

**FLESH** (Rom. 8:8)
The ingrained habit patterns still appeal to the mind to live independent of God.

*a human mind and the mind of the spirit*

**MIND**
Double-minded

**SPIRIT**
(Rom. 8:9)
Alive but quenched
(1 Thess. 5:19)

*the born again person has a spirit born of the Holy Spirit*

**BODY**
Tension or migraine headaches, nervous stomach, hives, skin rashes, allergies, asthma, some arthritis, spastic colon, heart palpitations, respiratory ailments, etc.

**EMOTIONS**
Unstable

*driven by the natural man - the old unregenerated man*

*but the sons of God are led by the Holy Spirit*

*Fruits of the flesh; flesh and blood cannot enter the kingdom of God*

walk after the flesh (often)
- immorality
- impurity
- sensuality
- idolatry
- sorcery
- enmities
- strife
- jealousy
- outbursts of anger
- disputes
- dissensions
- factions
- envying
- drunkenness
- carousing

walk after the Spirit (seldom)

*Fruits of the Spirit*
- love
- joy
- peace
- patience
- kindness
- goodness
- faithfulness
- gentleness
- self-control

*https://citizenheaven.wordpress.com*

# PART I: HUMAN BODY

## Understanding The Purpose of Your Body

When God created a man, he formed his body from the lower part of the earth. He created the triune being with spirit and soul in his likeness and body (mankind) being uniquely formed to carry out God activities on earth. The human body was created by God to be the home of your spirit (which is the real you), and the soul (which is the home of your thoughts, imaginations, and creativity). It must be made clear that God created the human body for his work purposes. As a matter of fact, God owns your body, and he gives and takes as he likes. When God created the earth, he gave its responsibility and dominion to mankind to extend his rulership on earth through us. But this rulership was to be done through consultation with God. This rulership was violated by mankind when they rebelled against God and sided with Satan. As the result of Satan's deception and rulership over mankind, God had to reduce our lifespan or the lifespan of our bodies on earth from immortality to mortality. Instead of forever bodies, they were reduced to one hundred twenty (120) years on earth because of the curse of our great grandfather Adam.

When Christ came, our bodies were redeemed through his blood, and forgiveness of sins reverted our bodies to the previous immortality, until when he comes to rule for one thousand years on earth. Through redemption, the rulership had to change when mankind's relationship with God was restored through the death of his son on the cross for our sins. As a result of this the rulership of the human bodies= they changed from being a mechanism of work to being the temple of the holy spirit. The spirit of God is now the owner of our body and he dwells in it. And if your body is the temple of the holy spirit then it must be holy as God is holy.

St. Paul made this assertion to the church of Corinth when people were misusing their bodies, particularly for prostitution. But not only that, they had failed in their unconditional love for others. As Christ has loved us, they failed in loving poor sinners, and ultimately loving themselves by dishonouring their bodies. He had to let them know that the spirit of God dwells in every believer's body and one has no right to it as he so chooses. As the rules of engagement changed between God and mankind, the spirit of God who now dwells in us has to counsel, convict, guide, remind and direct our work with God. When we are to do God's work, we must have the power of the holy spirit working in us to follow his instructions. St. Paul, while referring to our bodies as the temples of the holy spirit, was also talking about the church as a big Christian community of believers. It is the holy spirit who draws people together to form a big Christian community which is the church. It is our responsibility as Christians to build up the church of God. We must use the gifts of the holy spirit given to each one of us for the greater good of the people of God. For example, if one is blessed by God with one of the gifts of the holy spirit such as wisdom, administration, healing, and prophecy they must be shared to strengthen the church of God.

When the spirit of God lives in us, it gives us a sense of identity in God. He is always with us in good or bad situations. When this happens, he belongs to us and we belong to him. He comforts and guides us in building up our life of faith in Jesus Christ. Our faith must be built in the strong foundation of the word of God. Because it is our strength in good or bad times. When we are connected to Jesus Christ our salvation is guaranteed and our peaceful living here on earth is enjoyable. But this life only comes when we are committed to the things of God through prayers, fasting and bible study. When the holy spirit is the builder of our temple, the boundaries of hatred, jealousy, wars, race, and violence are removed from our hearts. Our love for others becomes limitless as the love of Christ attracts those who are seeking a better community of believers. We must treat people equally regardless of where they come from and how they look.

Overall, the important aspect of us being the temple of the holy spirit is to have unwavering faith in God and the things of God. Because of the spirit of God who lives in us, he keeps us closer to God. Through the spirit of God, our relationship with Jesus Christ is strengthened to be generous to the needy, to pray for those who are persecuted, the forgiveness of enemies and never pay back evil with evil. Because of Jesus Christ, God has created for himself one body of believers, no longer Jews, or gentiles.

# CHAPTER 1:

## THE HUMAN BODY IS WONDERFULLY MADE BY GOD

There is a battle over the origin of mankind and his body between the two versions of creation. The first account of the creation of the human body is written by God himself through his prophets inspired by the holy spirit. The second account of the creation of the human body is written by scientists inspired by their beliefs. These two accounts of the creation of the human body have confused many people today more than ever before. Many people have taken the version of the bible as a truly credible source of mankind's body origin. Many others have taken science as the truly credible source of the origin of mankind. These versions will be discussed in detail below before I take a stand on one of them. Even though there are divergent views about who created the human body, there is an agreement by those versions that it was formed out of the dust of the ground. Yes, the bible says that the body was formed out of the ground, but it was done by God. Science says that it was formed out of the ground through the unseen tiny particles that became human molecules which resulted in a body but not created by God. So one version says there is a creator of the human body, but the other one says there is no creator of the human body. I will show you the merits of both arguments below and you will have to decide which version is correct just as I did a few years back.

## The Bible Version of the Creation of Your Body

When God said, "*let us create mankind in our image*", he created first the spiritual us (mankind)- because God is a spirit, so he had to create the spirit-us first. After the creation of the human spirit, he created our souls (mind, emotions, and wills). After the creation of the souls of mankind, he had to create the tent in which we live, which is the body out of the soil of the ground. After the creation was complete, God had to wrap both the spirit-person, soul-person, and body-person into the woman's womb resulting in pregnancy. This assertion is proven in the book of the prophet Jeremiah 1:4-5-*"Then the word of the Lord came to me, saying: "Before I formed you in the womb, I knew you; Before you were born I sanctified you; I ordained you a prophet to the nations."* These verses show that the prophet Jeremiah existed before he was formed in his mother's womb as a foetus according to science. Furthermore, God had given a job description to Jeremiah before he was even conceived. It is another indication that God gives people their job before they are born, and for this reason, you must stop chasing other people's calls and seek God for your calls.

Furthermore, in the book of *Psalms 139:13-16,* *"For You formed my inward parts: You covered me in my mother's womb. I will praise You, for I am fearfully and wonderfully made; marvellous are Your works, and that my soul knows very well. My frame was not hidden from You when I was made in secret and skillfully wrought in the lowest parts of the earth. Your eyes saw my substance, being yet unformed. And in Your book, they all were written, the days fashioned for me when as yet there were none of them."* David seems to indicate in these verses that God knew him before he was even created as both spirit, soul and body. This means that God knew him as an idea in his mind before he became a human being. So, God had an idea that became a human being before David was even created and conceived in the womb (before people could see the pregnancy in the womb). The use of the personal pronouns in these verses mean that there was an actual King David in existence as a person before he was born.

Another scripture in support of the existence of life before birth is in the book of Luke 1:39-44- *"Now Mary arose in those days and went into the hill country with haste, to a city of Judah, and entered the house of Zacharias and greeted Elizabeth. And it happened, when Elizabeth heard the greeting of Mary, that the baby leapt in her womb; and Elizabeth was filled with the Holy Spirit. Then she spoke out with a loud voice and said, 'Blessed are you among women, and blessed is the fruit of your womb! But why is this granted to me, that the mother of my Lord should come to me? For indeed, as soon as the voice of your greeting sounded in my ears, the baby leapt in my womb for joy.'"* Here in these verses, there is proof that human beings do exist before they are born. These two great women of God met and the baby (John) in the womb of her mother Elizabeth leapt in her because of joy being experienced by Elizabeth. This was in the presence of her God in her house in the like of Mary with the baby Jesus in her womb. These verses indicate that God considers the unborn baby as a fully complete human being before birth. Because of this simple reason the spirits are the same – that one of a child and that one of an adult. All the spirits do not grow, age, or die.

Certainly, with these verses in mind, it is reasonable to believe that life starts before conception in the womb of a woman. The human being exists first as an idea in God's mind with the specific assignment to carry out here on earth before he or she is conceived in the womb of a woman. That is why God considers you a murderer when you kill an unborn child. Abortion is a sin in the eyes of God. Killing the unborn child is just like killing an adult human being because they are equal in God's eyes. This claim is also supported in the book of Exodus 21:22-24: *"If men fight, and hurt a woman with child, so that she gives birth prematurely, yet no harm follows, he shall surely be punished accordingly as the woman's husband imposes on him; and he shall pay as the judges determine. But if any harm follows, then you shall give life for life, eye for an eye, tooth for tooth, hand for hand, foot for foot".* The harm noted in these verses refers to the child and not the mother who is pregnant with the child. A fine could be levied if two men fight and injure the pregnant mother that may result in premature birth. But if as a result of injury of the pregnant mother ended in the child dead, then the penalty is life for life-so both men or one of them can be killed as a result of the death of the child. That is how serious God is about the unborn baby. God even put it further; if you kill the unborn child intentionally you should be killed as an adult. So, the bible is absolutely clear with nothing suggesting that the unborn child is less important in comparison to the fully grown-up human being from the moment it is conceived in the womb to the time it is born. We have looked at these verses of the bible and nothing seems to suggest that God is not the sole creator of the human body.

# The Scientific Version of the Creation of Your Body

When it comes to the formation of the human body, science and the bible seems to agree that the human body is formed out of the soil of the ground. But when it comes to the soul and spirit (the important parts of human beings), scientists and theologians have divergent views. The bible scholars believe that human beings are both a spirit and soul that lives in the body which is the tent. While scientists do not have definite clear-cut explanations on the spirit and soul as important parts of human beings, instead they base their studies heavily on the human body. There are no clear scientific studies of the human development process right from the time of non-existence of the foetus to the time of conception until the time of childbirth, that point to the creation of human beings. Besides, there is no custodian or solo creator of the human being, according to scientific studies. Much research has been done looking at the electrical activity of the human body, chemical processes and changes in shape and size of the human body and stages of a human being's maturation. These have been studied but all in vain, not answering these important questions: When does the life of a human being start? How does it start? What is the composition of it? It is shocking that with this great field of human study called science there no clear explanation over how a human being is formed.

All we have seen is the process of the formation of an embryo (Zygote, foetus, baby), into the human being after the sexual intercourse between male and female, resulting in pregnancy in the womb of a woman. But that is it, there is nothing beyond this talking about the spirit of mankind. Even with the vast knowledge that seems to dominate almost all areas of human society, science has just continued to reveal human developmental processes in three stages: conception, maturation in the womb of a woman and childbirth. These stages flow continuously from one to the next in precision. The more we study these stages the more they demand more explanations and answers. The fundamental question remains: When does human life start?

Most of the scientists do agree that human life begins at conception. This literally means that when two people, male and female, have sexual intercourse, it results in a conception. But this looks to me as a shallow explanation of how the human being came about. You cannot just define a human being who has a body, soul, and spirit in these simple terms. It is shockingly unbelievable that science which has shown us the wonderful continuity of the development of human life in all stages is unable to tell us completely – when does human life begin? It looks like science cannot answer this question so let us return to the bible to look for answers to this question. The answer to this question must go beyond human conception.

There is a clear explanation in the bible that human beings are the composition of spirit, soul, and body. We know that both spirit and soul are created in God's image and the body out of the soil of the ground all wrapped into the woman's womb to form a human being. So, when the bible speaks of the unborn it speaks of the already formed human being in the woman's womb. So, to be exact God is the beginning of the creation of the human being in the womb, not when two people, male and female have intercourse that results in conception (pregnancy). It is clearly convincing that human creation starts first in the supernatural (unseen world) before it appears in the natural (seen world).

Certainly, out of these two world views (science and religion), a conclusion could be made that the life of the human being does not begin in the womb or at birth, but the way in eternity with God before birth. But not only that, the assignment we are so passionate about today in the world starts from eternity as well, as we have seen in the case of the prophet Jeremiah. God the creator of all things is not only the creator of human beings he is also responsible for their assignments. In short, you are created with what to do.

So, this question could be asked – Is abortion (killing of the unborn child) a sin? Having looked at both perspectives of religion and science the answer is yes – it is a sin. No matter what altruistic reason may be given for the abortion, destroying an embryo is murder. In agreement, science has told us that a human being's life starts in the womb, whereas the word of God, the Bible, tells us that life starts before the womb and that abortion is a crime. In fact, the Bible is unequivocally clear that God created human beings in his own image and thereafter continue to reproduce in his own image. It also tells us that God is serious about what we do to the unborn children. Above all God sent his son into the whole world to die for our own sins including the unborn babies.

Which is the true version of the creation of the human body, bible or science?

It must be made clear that God is the creator and the owner of your body. For the simple reason, to date, science does not claim the creation of anything on earth including the human body but rather claims the invention and discovery of God's creations. So, in short, God creates and science discovers. Science explains God's creation and it must remain so. Many scientists are tempted today to dismiss the existence of God, yet the scientist of the 16th, 17th and 18th centuries believed in God. For instance, the words "created and creation," appear in the bible on numerous occasions indicating that God almighty is the Lord of creation. This fact must be accepted by scientists and the world at large. The concept of evolution was an ill-informed series of lies by men influenced by Satan to distract mankind from their creator. In being fair to the science world there are some scientists who have rejected evolution as they see it accurately and objectively to be baseless. But the establishment of this world; universities, courts, schools, workplaces, written books, news media, false religion, rich businessmen, politicians, and kings attempt to dismiss the teaching of the bible and those who believe in it. They have perverted, discredited, and removed the bible and its teaching from all the areas of our human society today. It is not a secret that people who believe in God are getting intimidated, accused, abused, tortured, and even executed in some countries. The next generation is the target as bible teaching is being removed from the schools and written books or even in the worst scenario being discredited as not a true account of the origin of the world and mankind. You can see this for example, in many areas of society today; politics is taken over by secularism (the worshipping of what you want rather than God); Media is taken over by lies and false opinions polls that do not reflect the true opinions of people who elect their leaders; Science is taken over by scientists who deny the existence of God and greed by scientists who do no longer care about the health of people but their own interests through the manufacturing of harmful drugs for money; Church has been taken over by same-sex marriage, sexual assault maniacs who do not view them as sins; society is taken over by division and rejection of our other fellow human beings, and business is taken over by a few corrupt individuals who make people pay mortgages for life plus much more. All of these should serve as a red flag for you by now. The moment we disown God in our human society there is always a disaster that hits us. As was the case in the time of Noah because most of the human beings who were created by God, no longer appreciated God and his marvellous works of creation – he responded by wiping them off the earth and he started all over again.

It is even getting harder for Christians today to stand up against abortion, gay marriage, and climate change as moral issues of this time – yet these are based on the lies of Satan. You could see today; a woman being told that she is the master of her body and she can do what she wants with it including the child she is pregnant with. Yet we know that our bodies are the temple of the holy spirit according to the bible. It seems that the world has been taken over by science and particularly the concept of evolution. It seems that people have been made to believe this lie and they are believing it as a true source of the origin of the world. The worrying thing is that people no longer repent of their sins, which leads to their death. For if the person does not repent and believe in Jesus Christ as the source of his or her salvation, they are destined for hell.

# CHAPTER 2:

## THE BODY AS A TEMPLE OF THE HOLY SPIRIT

Let me make this statement; you cannot understand the importance of your body until you understand its purpose. God created your body for his purpose, not your purpose. So, your body is not yours but God's. God created your body as a temple of his spirit (Holy Spirit).

Let me make another important statement; for spirits to work or operate here on earth they need a body. That is why the holy spirit of God, which is the God-head representative here on earth, needs your body as his residence. Without a human body all spirits, holy spirit (God) and evil spirit (Satan) can do nothing here on earth. That makes your body a battleground for control by either a good spirit or bad spirit.

Unless you get this, you will never understand how the spiritual world operates. Therefore, you must be accountable to God, in the way you control your body under his authority and power. Every single one of us as Christians can have his or her body under the absolute control of God once they accept Jesus Christ as their personal saviour. God has given us the responsibility to rule over all the residence/temple of the Holy Spirit, including our thoughts, actions, deeds, imaginations, creativities, and desires on behalf of God.

## Old Temple

We perhaps may not fully understand what the temple is until we look at its history. So, what does it really mean that our bodies are temples of the holy spirit? Let us see how the Israelites used to worship. In the Old Testament, the temple was the sacred place set aside by the Israelites to worship their God. They worshipped there to God, made sacrifices there for their sins to God, and presented their requests to God for healing and blessings. It was during Solomon's reign as king, (the son of King David), that the Israelites built a temple for their God.

Previously, the Israelites had a tabernacle of God. In God's commands to Moses, *"Then have them make a sanctuary for me, and I will dwell among them."* In Exodus, God spells out very clearly the instructions for building the tabernacle and detailing out exactly what he wanted his tabernacle to look like with complicated designs, gold, and silver. It was really a mark of greatest honour to God. The tabernacle was not just beautiful but also holy. It was holy to such an extent that you could not go into the place called holy of holies without blood in your hands as a Priest (Aaron) or else you would be dead. Furthermore, it was so holy that when a man called Uzzah reached out to reposition the ark so it would not fall because the tabernacle was being moved and an ox had stumbled, he was immediately struck and killed by God for his irreverence. Accordingly, many scholars have said over the years, that the purpose of the tabernacle was to be a movable place where heaven met earth so that God could commune with his people unobstructed by sin. Wherever the Israelites went, God wanted to go with them to comfort and to direct them. This was the true reason why it was built beside the fact that the Israelites had not yet had a place to call home before the possession of their promised land. That was how dangerous it was to misuse the temple and let us now look at how dangerous it is to misuse the temple.

## Modern Temple
## (Your Body as a Residence of the Holy Spirit of God)

That was the historical context of the temple but when Jesus came, he eliminated the need for a temple being in a single location. Christians became the temple of God, a house for his Holy Spirit. Because of his blood that made us clean, we can now be considered pure and holy enough to have God's Spirit lives in us. We have become a meeting place between heaven and earth to bring other people into commune with God. Since we are now a sacred house, a holy ground, nothing unclean or defiling should have its presence within us. In other words, no Christian should engage in sin, iniquity, and transgression against God in his temple (mankind). Galatians 5-19 *"Now the works of the flesh are manifest, which are these; Adultery, fornication, uncleanness, lasciviousness, idolatry, witchcraft, hatred, violence, emulations, wrath, strife, seditions, heresies, envy, murder, drunkenness, revellings, and such like: of which I tell you, as I have also told you in time past, that they which do such things shall not inherit the kingdom of God".* When Jesus Christ came, everything changed from visibility into invisibility. From the visible temple (building) to the invisible temple (mankind/human beings). From the laws of God written on the stone to laws of God written in our hearts. Someone may ask why God has done this? And the answer is; because we used to access him physically (we had no faith) as we never knew him and now, we have known him, and we can access him by faith. Without faith, it is impossible to please him.

In the letter St Paul wrote to the church in Corinth around 55 AD (after the death of Christ),-he rebukes the church over many issues, settling law disputes outside the church, sexual immorality, eating foods given to idols, and incest (having sex with close members of the family). Sexual immorality was rampant and prevalent in Corinth to the extent that a son would sleep with his father's wife. Ultimately and evidently, the church in Corinth was struggling in their sexual immoralities, and St Paul is using the concept of the temple to address it. But this message is not to the Corinthians alone but to us today as Christians and the followers of Jesus Christ. Paul implores us to recognise that our bodies are not our own but belong to God. Having been bought at a price by Jesus Christ's death and resurrection, as stated, we do not have any right to give them over to sin (sexual immorality in the case of Corinthians, and to us today in the context of homosexuality, pornography, abortion, and prostitution). All these acts defile God's temple and not only that but also grieve the spirit of God within you. As a matter of fact, it is impossible for the holy spirit to live in these sin infested temples, and he may be obliged to leave. It is a fearful thing for the spirit of God to leave you as St James; puts it; a body without the spirit is dead. Christians may feel that it is their freedom to use their bodies according to what they want to do with it but know that we are slaves to the righteousness of God. We were delivered from the slavery of sin (Satan) to the slavery of righteousness (God). Yes, this may sound like we have no freedom at all, but we are slaves of sins to (death) and slaves of righteousness to salvation (life). Therefore, we should keep our minds on things from above giving us life as opposed to things on earth giving us temptations leading to death. When we accept Jesus Christ as our Saviour, we have no right to do whatever we choose to do with our bodies. The major difference between Christianity and other religions of the world is the presence of the spirit of God within us. The bible tells very clearly that without the presence of the spirit of God in us we will never, understand the deep things of God, receive revelations, teach the bible, raise the dead, heal the sick and cast out demons. So, without the holy spirit, we are nothing. As Christians, we must acknowledge the holy spirit of God within us in what we do to our bodies and the words we speak to ourselves and others, as a special God-head representative here on earth, sealed to us from the beginning of the creation for our salvation. So, you can see the importance of the holy spirit being within us.

Without the holy spirit (God Wisdom), mankind will have zero communication with God. If you do not have the spirit of God in you, you are not a child of God. Another hard fact. There is nothing in between, either you are with the devil or with God!!! Human beings have no middle ground. Because there is something beyond its wisdom.

It is through the holy spirit that we as Christians, are deeply grounded and rooted in the things of God. All the information from the kingdom of God flows through him to us. It is through holy spirit revelations to us that the true meaning of words of the bible can be understood. It is through the holy spirit that we become children of God. He is the Godhead (God the Father, God the Son, and God the holy spirit), representative here on earth. The Holy Spirit is known by various names, including the Spirit of God, the Spirit of truth, and the finger of God. His roles among Christians are to; comfort, convict, advocate, guide, counsel and help children of God overcome the daily challenges the devil presents to them.

Ephesians 4:30 – *"**And do not grieve the holy spirit of God, with whom you were sealed for the day of redemption**"*. This practically means that the holy spirit can be annoyed, resisted, and disappointed by Christians because he is a person and has feelings. Watch this, the new covenant under our lord Jesus is unlike the old covenant of Moses which was law. Judgements and commandments of God were written on stone; now instead, the laws, judgements, and commandments of God are written in people's hearts and minds. It means that you and I are left with no excuse of later on saying, Oh Lord I did not hear or know about the Kingdom. For example, in every language, every tradition, in every culture no one can claim not to have heard of or know God. Also, practically as a person, you wrestle daily between what is good and what is evil in your hearts and minds. For example, if you choose what is evil when you are aroused to anger, the holy spirit will convict you afterwards and you will come to realise that you have committed a crime. That is a work of the holy spirit practically in you. His job is to guide you away from sin but when you overrule him, he will convict you later. So, he is your first protector before the armies and police of the nations. He is also your judge before the judges of the world. So, if you live respecting the voice of the holy spirit inside you, you will never commit any crime. And if you commit a crime and later repent of It, he will go and represent you in the court of law to enable you to speak powerful words you will even admit as not your own.

Jesus Christ, who was a hundred per cent human being became a hundred per cent God through his baptism with the holy spirit. It is important to note that the holy spirit descended on him in the form of a dove accompanying the voice saying, **"He is my son with whom I am well pleased"**. He was the absolute power Jesus relied on to preach the gospel to the people, nations, and kingdoms of the world. Quote, **"The**

*Spirit of the Lord is upon me because He has anointed me to preach the gospel to the poor; He has sent me to heal the broken-hearted, to proclaim liberty to the captives and recovery of sight to the blind, to set at liberty those who are oppressed".*

## How Do You Allow the Holy Spirit to Operate Through You?

The holy spirit can be activated through a believer by a prayer. Luke 11:13 *"If you then, being evil, know how to give good gifts to your children, how much more will your heavenly Father give the Holy Spirit to those who ask Him!"* He can also be imparted to a believer through the laying on of hands by a pastor who has the anointing of the holy spirit. Where the spirit of God is there is freedom, and through him, you are able to pray to God according to God's will and it is also through him that you are able to forgive other people who have wronged you. It is through the power of the holy spirit that you are filled with hope if everything around you is against you and about to take you out. If the holy spirit is in you, you will never be sick, and if you are sick you will be healed.    I Corinthians 6:19-20- *"Do you not know that your bodies are the temple of the holy spirit, who is in you, who you have received from God? You are not your own; you were bought at a price. therefore, honour God with your bodies."* It is when you are filled with the holy spirit that you can preach the gospel of Jesus Christ to the poor, captives, limbless, blind and the deaf. It is through the power of the holy spirit that you can cast out demons, heal the sick, speak in tongues and hold serpents with your hands and they will not by any means harm you.

## Satan Wants Your Temple
## (Your Body as a Residence of Evil Spirits)

Never give Satan a chance to destroy the temple of God. He is up to no good at all. He will overuse your body and eventually will kill you. John 10:10- *"The thief does not come except to steal, and to kill, and to destroy. I have come that they may have life and that they may have it more abundantly".* So, it is God who can give you life and he can give it more abundantly. 1 Corinthians 6:9-11- *"Do you not know that the unrighteous will not inherit the kingdom of God? Do not be deceived. Neither fornicators, nor idolaters, nor adulterers, nor homosexuals, nor sodomites, nor thieves, nor the covetous, nor drunkards, nor revellers, nor extortioners will inherit the kingdom of God. And such were some of you. But you were washed, but you were sanctified, but you were justified in the name of the Lord Jesus and by the Spirit of our God".* There is nothing God hates like sins. Never allow sin to rule in the body as it is from the devil, and it will eventually lead to your death. In other words, what many Christians do not know is that a life of sins blocks God's blessings for you and your family. In short, if you want God's blessings then keep away from sins and if you have committed one, just admit it, repent of it and return to God. Never repeat it again as it will be testing God. When you test God, you are no longer liable for forgiveness, but judgement. It is a fearful thing to fall into the hands of God. Never allow the devil to have a stronghold within you. God said, *"If your right eye causes you to sin, pluck it out and throw it away for it is better for you to enter God's kingdom with one eye than to lose your salvation with two eyes that will prevent your salvation".* As a matter of fact, do not put yourself in an environment that puts you at risk of engaging in sins and all forms of lawlessness. Things such as alcohol abuse, drug dealings and abuse, all forms of sexual immorality, hatred, skin bleaching, abortion, racism, and pornography – keep yourself and your family out of them and avoid places where they can be easily obtained.

Over years now since modern communities, society and traditions have often promoted unnatural standards for beauty and looking young, particularly with the need for science and technology. Science and technology have done more damage to human society than one can imagine. Starting from genetically modified food, skin bleaching cream, weapons of mass destruction (WMD), immoral sexual television programmes, sexual pornographic websites, and internet scamming online activities that have caused people to commit suicide. Because of old age, we find our bodies changing in ways such as the appearance of wrinkles and grey hairs, or the lack of muscular volume we have seen on a celebrity, so we may see our bodies as nothing but problems that need to be fixed. But take note of this, nothing we put into our bodies from outside will replace and fix what God has already put in there. Let nobody lie to you that they can replace what God has done. This is demonic thinking that needs to be eliminated or rebuked. God says; **"We are fearfully and wonderfully made"** (Psalm 139:14). Satan will attempt to use our insecurities over our weight, beauty, or age to distract us from our call-to spread the Gospel to all the corners of the world as Jesus Christ has asked us to do. But if we view our bodies as a creation of the most high God, we can combat this distraction from our calling and purpose on earth. Throughout history, the Israelites, upon turning away from God, used their temple as a place of idols. For example, they set up an idol to Zeus in the temple, and money changers turned Jesus' temple into a den of thieves where they were trading. In other words, they turned the temple of God into a business centre. Whenever idols and idols worshipping entered the temple of God, it aroused God's anger against the Israelites, and to us today, causing destruction. The Jews got rid of the statue of Zeus after the Maccabean revolt. Manasseh removed the idols, and Jesus overturned tables all as a punishment. One way to treat our bodies like a temple is to get rid of the idols within them. Remove the idols that we have placed within it, as it is the temple of the Holy Spirit of God. We can never have two masters ruling our bodies at the same time. What does removing idols within our bodies mean? Literally, it means removing items that deteriorate or affect our health or well-being such as smoking, skin bleaching, binge drinking, drug abuse, abortion, pornographic activities. These are all works of Satan to destroy you.

Satan has deceived the whole world. He started with Eve and Adam at the garden of Eden. And too, later followed suit with the offspring of Adam. He gets them to doubt God, mistrust God, blame God and to question God's existence. He causes people to trust in the things of this world. This is the greatest distraction he has done. Instead of Christians going to the church on Sundays, he gets them to watch movies, football, political campaigns, and other social functions. So, Sunday becomes a day for human pleasure not for worshipping God. He causes people to accept false Gospels, false writings, false prophecies, false prophets, false visions, false religions, false preachers, false priests. He deceives people to believe in philosophy, psychology, astrology, and evolution as their God. To them, the idea that there is a living God is unrealistic and out of touch. They are uncomfortable with what they cannot see and test in the laboratory. And none of this is true. We as human beings did not come from apes; that is a big fat lie. For those that believe the Bible, Satan distorts its meanings in their hearts and minds. Satan also deceives Christians through riches, prosperity, cares of this life, the lusts of other things and the pleasures of this life. He uses a person's doubts, desires, depression, rejection, anger, fear, jealousy, envy, covetousness, and unforgiveness to draw them away from God and His Word.

Throughout the earth, Satan deceives many Christians and non-Christians, using radio, television, the internet, magazines, books, clergy, religions, churches, organisations, associations, businesses, local leaders and government officials, and other people. His weapons of deception seem almost limitless. Satan is an expert at causing people to have wrong thinking. He is an expert in using a person's own emotions to his advantage. He is an expert at causing a person's emotions to fabricate lies while ignoring the truth. He is an expert in tempting and deceiving the entire earth. Satan puts lying thoughts into a person's mind, then their heart chooses to believe the lying thought, and the person becomes deceived. Satan is the father of lies. He destroys and was a murderer from the beginning as scriptures put it.

Today in many parts of the world the devil is being worshipped openly by magicians, diviners, sorcerers, and witchdoctors, through the offering of human sacrifice as people burn their sons and daughters in the fire to their gods. They also use important sites such as the high mountains and hills, under trees and the large water bodies, altars, sacred pillars, wooden images and carved images. This is most prevalent in the typical villages of the third world far from current human civilisation. Some traditions have also refused to let go of their gods after the incursion of Christianity into their societies and their villages. So, for those demonic sceptics, the devil is real just like the above evidence demonstrates. So, what do people mean when they say there is no God when there is a real Satan? Are we oblivious to the obvious or are we denying the truth?

Satan is also being worshipped internally (in people's heart's) by many Christians and non-Christians through human's hatred, jealousy, anger, greed, loathing, prostitution, drunkenness, homosexuality, stealing, murder, covertness, adultery and so much more. The irony is that none of us like these demonic weapons/wiles and darts, yet we practise them against ourselves as mankind. The day you will know that there is a real Satan in this world, is the day you will try to get rid of one of the above within you, and you will see the devil in his true colours. I dare you. That is why the bible says that we are all sinners because, whether you like it or not, we are children of the devil as alluded to by the scriptures above. Because none of us is free from one or two of those demonic weapons. Demons have a well organised and structured kingdom that uses the human body to operate. Without the human body, demons cannot carry out their activities. It is only through the baptism of (water) and baptism with the (holy spirit) of Christians, that God can thwart and completely stop the demonic activities in human beings. This will be shortly a subject of discussion.

## Demons Have Well-Organised Structures and Areas of Specialisations as Highlighted Below.

Demonic specialisation: Foul spirits (causing attacks against peoples using darts, and wiles)- Mark 9:25; Unclean Spirits (causing uncleanliness on people – violent, vomiting, foaming, convulsion)- Matthew 10:1; Spirit of fear (causing uncontrollable fear in people – failure, stress, depression) -2 Timothy 1:7; Seducing spirits (misleading people through religions and doctrines)-1 Timothy 4:1; Spirit of infirmity (causing sickness in the human body)- Luke 13:11; Spirit of divination ( prophecy and seeing into the future of people)- Acts 16:16; Spirit of bondage (slavery and possession of people); Romans 8:15 – Spirit of Slumber (causes laziness and poor concentration of people)- Romans 11:8; Spirit of the world (the ruler of the world) – 1 Corinthians 2:12; Spirit of Antichrist (causing people to reject Jesus Christ as a son of God)- 1 John 4:3; Miracle-working spirits (performing miracles to show their powers to lead people away from God) – Revelations:16:14; and finally, The Devourer Spirits (cause financial difficulty and poor agricultural harvests) – Malachi 3:11.

## Demonic Powers and Hierarchies of Rulers and Wickedness: Ephesians 6:12

The system of governance used by all governments of the world today is demonic. *1Samuel 8:1-22- "Now it came to pass when Samuel was old that he made his sons judges over Israel. The name of his firstborn was Joel, and the name of his second, Abijah; they were judges in Beersheba. But his sons did not walk in his ways; they turned aside after dishonest gain, took bribes, and perverted justice. Then all the elders of Israel gathered and came to Samuel at Ramah, and said to him, "Look, you are old, and your sons do not walk in your ways. Now make us a king to judge us like all the nations." But the thing displeased Samuel when they said, "Give us a king to judge us." So, Samuel prayed to the Lord. And the Lord said to Samuel, "Heed the voice of the people in all that they say to you; for they have not rejected you, but they have rejected Me, that I should not reign over them." According to all the works which they have done since the day that I brought them up out of Egypt, even to this day—with which they have forsaken Me and served other gods—so they are doing to you also. "Now, therefore, heed their voice. However, you shall solemnly forewarn them, and show them the behaviour of the king who will reign over them.* "*So, Samuel told all the words of the Lord to the people who asked him for a king. And he said,* "*This will be the behaviour of the king who will reign over you: He will take your sons and appoint them for his own chariots and to be his horsemen, and some will run before his chariots.* "*He will appoint captains over his thousands and captains over his fifties, will set some to plough his ground and reap his harvest, and some to make his weapons of war and equipment for his chariots.* "*He will take your daughters to be perfumers, cooks, and bakers.* "*And he will take the best of your fields, your vineyards, and your olive groves, and give them to his servants.* "*He will take a tenth of your grain and your vintage and give it to his officers and servants.* "*And he will take your male servants, your female servants, your finest young men, and your donkeys, and put them to his work.* "*He will take a tenth of your sheep. And you will be his servants.* "*And you will cry out in that day because of your king whom you have chosen for yourselves, and the LORD will not hear you in that day.*" *Nevertheless, the people refused to obey the voice of Samuel; and they said,* "*No, but we will have a king over us,* "*that we also may be like all the nations, and that our king may judge us and go out before us and fight our battles*". *And Samuel heard all the words of the people, and he repeated them in the hearing of the Lord. So, the Lord said to Samuel,* "*Heed their voice, and make them a king.*" *And Samuel said to the men of Israel,* "*Every man goes to his city.*"

It is important to note that the responsibility of naming everything on earth, both living and non-living was given to Adam by God, which Satan took over when Adam got deceived by him. So, it is Satan through mankind, who divided the earth into continents, regions, and principalities. Principalities (regions) – Strong and powerful demons oversee the parts of the world. Notable large territories: Powers (The systems of hell). Power is distributed to demons according to the regions they control. This is from smaller and to the bigger hierarchies of the demonic powers possessed by each demon; Rulers of the darkness of this world (Demonic spiritual beings), the demons that wander the earth and Spiritual wickedness in the high places (fallen angels) the one-third of the angels which were cast down with Satan and remain unchained. They are based in the second heaven beyond human eyes.

## This is How the Devil Can Torment a Person

To enter the human body demons, look for open doors (drugs, ungodly music, pornography, demonic rituals, excessive anger, quarrels); distraction (watching movies and football on Sunday); depression (sadness, relationships problems and divorce), intimidation (assault on people or wiles to instil fear); deception (words – believing what people say without questioning); temptation (lust of the eyes, lust of the flesh and the pride of life); accusation (sin – wrongdoing).

The beauty of God's kingdom is that nobody is coerced into believing in it, but rather we are given a choice whether to serve him or the devil. The choices are very clear; it is either God's kingdom or the demonic kingdom. Nothing is in between for mankind; it is either heaven or hell. My job is to make these choices abundantly clear as much as possible.

# CHAPTER 3:

## THE BODY AS A MECHANISM OF WORK

God has already determined your vision and mission here on earth if you are a Christian. That looks like good news to you, but the bad news is that you cannot achieve it without the help of God, because the devil knows it better than you do, and he is against it. "Work". We must work or else we cannot have God's blessings. If you do not work, then forget about God's blessings. New King James Version 2 Thessalonians 3:8,10-12; *"Nor did we eat anyone's bread free of charge, but worked with labour and toil night and day, that we might not be a burden to any of you, for even when we were with you, we commanded you this: If anyone will not work, neither shall he eat. For we hear that there are some who walk among you in a disorderly manner, not working at all, but are busybodies. Now those who are such we command and exhort through our Lord Jesus Christ that they work in quietness and eat their own bread".*

God created human beings to work for him. The difference between you and God is your body, which was created for work. You must work for God to bless the work of your hands. In fact, this claim is supported in all the books of the bible and particularly in the book of Genesis, where God did not send rain on earth because there were no humans to till and plough the ground. **(New King James Version) Genesis 2:5:** *Before any plant of the field was in the earth and before any herb of the field had grown. For the Lord God had not caused it to rain on the earth, and there was no man to till the ground."*

If you want God's blessings, then you must work. *"Then to Adam, He said, "Because you have heeded the voice of your wife and have eaten from the tree of which I commanded you, saying, 'You shall not eat of it: "Cursed is the ground for your sake; In toil, you shall eat of it all the days of your life.*(Genesis 3:17). NJKV.

Some people have claimed these verses at times saying there are no jobs because the governments and businesses have not provided them jobs. Yes, indeed there may be an element of truth to it but listen to me very carefully; no governments and businesses will work for your interests. Treat them as a ladder in the short term to, later on, do your own thing in life. You are not free until you do your own thing. You are not happy until you do your own thing. On top of that, the businesses we seek employment from today were once established by people like us.

## Spirit of Entrepreneurism

This brings me to the spirit of entrepreneurism. People who establish their own things in life are people who find themselves with fountains of ideas wallowing inside them. What you are passionate about and have your desires to do is your God-given gift. Follow your heart on what you want to do in life, and you will see the wonders of the God-given gift inside you exploding into bigger things that will blow away your mind. Look internally within you and you will have no one coming against you because they will be coming against what is not their God-given gift. **(New King James Version) Romans 12:6-8:** *Having then gifts differing according to the grace that is given to us, let us use them: if prophecy, let us prophecy in proportion to our faith; or ministry, let us use it in our ministering; he who teaches, in teaching; he who exhorts, in exhortation; he who gives, with liberality; he who leads, with diligence; he who shows mercy, with cheerfulness.*

Consider the following four factors of production; land, labour, capital and entrepreneurship and you will never lack what to do in life. Where your hands (Labour) are available to you to work, use them. Where the land is the only thing available to you to work, cultivate it. Where your ideas are the only thing available to you, use them. Where your money is the only thing available to you, use it to establish a business. So, no excuse for not working at all.

## We Are Born as Problem Solving Beings

God cannot do anything on earth without human beings, and human beings cannot do anything on earth without God. Partnership!!! Get this fact and it will change your life for good, including your thinking about God. God is not going to do things for you unilaterally without your cooperation. Otherwise, your prayer to him must be meaningless. This statement may not sit well with many people, but that is okay, that is why I am an independent-minded person.

This has come as a blind spot to many people, as they think that life without problems is a good life. If you are one of these people, then you are deadly wrong. Problems are there as a part of your God-given assignment and destiny. The problems you are going through, have nothing to do with your sins being bigger than other people's sins just to justify what you are going through as your mistake. Trials are there as part of God's assignment for your life. God will build your faith up through the trials you are going through. You must learn to face them and fix them or else they will continue to flood to you like water. It is only when you know how to fix the problems, that Satan will stop bringing them to you. It does not matter what kind and type of the problem/problems you are in – whether it is sickness, poverty, unemployment, barrenness, drought, fire, flood, storms, accident, imprisonment, depression, blood pressure, family separation, job loss, you name it. Whatever the problem/problems you are going through, remember that God is at your doorstep. Allow him in. The are there (problems), to tell you that, what you are comfortable doing is not what God wants you to do, and you must be awakened for real assignment.

Think about this, no great single person in the living memory of the world has not fixed a certain problem. In human history: Abraham Lincoln and the problem of racism and slavery in America and the world at large. Martin Luther Jr King and the problem of civil rights in America and the world. Nelson Mandela and the problem of apartheid and racism in South Africa. Winston Churchill and the problem of empires and imperialism in the world. This is just to name a few, and the list continues. In the Bible, Moses had the problem of bondage and slavery of the Hebrews in Egypt. Joseph had the problem of starvation of both the Egyptian and Hebrews in Egypt. Abraham had the problem of God's lineage on earth to save human beings and faith, and Paul had the problem of the Jew and gentile separation and God's laws. The list could continue. Hence, you must focus on the problems of the world and you will never miss what to do. Looks at the problems of the career you have chosen or are about to choose and you will hit the ground running with your God-calling. If you are a politician focused on the fundamental problems of human society, you will never miss your God-given assignment; If you are a lawyer focused on the problems of laws you will never miss your God-given assignment; If you are a businessman focused on the problems of business, you will never miss your God-given assignment. Problems!! Problems!! Problems!!! are there in your life and that of others to allow you to fix them?

## Two Types of Workplace Problems: Addiction or Disappointment

It is either that someone loves his job too much that he does not want to leave it, or someone hates his job too much that he wants to leave it. If someone is at either end of the two faces of addiction or disappointment there are signs of eternity absent-mindedness, as their work becomes more important than their God who put them there. If you are a Christian, know that it is God who places you at the place of work for a particular purpose and you must seek his will before or after your condition of either hopefulness or hopelessness over your job. In the case of our job addiction or disappointment, God is ready to meet us there; his grace protects our hearts and opens our eyes to see what is eternal and valuable to us at these difficult moments of our lives.

The workplace addiction is caused by the following: position and power, relationships, payment, connection, and career advancement that become the small gods we worship. As one begins to worship their work, they are giving it all their available time, and as they do this, their other responsibilities including family times with their spouse and children begin to struggle or suffer. If one is a Christian, one's relationship with God begins to suffer as well. Central to a person's heart is their work that has been made of greater value than other responsibilities in their lives. From this point, forward work becomes a person's life-giver whether they recognise it or not. The power and position of the workplace slowly begin to destroy the person and other important things of his or her life. The workplace addiction can be fatal to people who cannot balance it with their other responsibilities.

In today's world disappointment at work may come from; lack of promotion; payment cut, boss intimidation and harassment, bad performance review, unfulfilled promises, and disloyal and bullying co-workers. When this happens to you, your hopes and aspirations with that particular company are crushed and your heart begins to shift into another place of work where you will work comfortably with lesser thorns, frustration, bullying, harassment, and progression of your career. At moments like this if you are a Christian, it is important to look at work through the correct lenses as not who you are, and not the final ends of your life. It is from here that you must view your work in the concept of eternity. When you view your work from God's perspective you will begin to understand that your work is part of your calling and not your life; your work gives you dignity but not your hope; and finally, work is not your final destination but part of your journey to your final destination. Workplace frustration can be fatal if we are not Christian and if we are Christian then we must always trust God in whatever situations we find ourselves in.

We must view our work in the concept of eternity as both our physical work and pleasure times are balanced according to God's perspective. We must focus on what the bible says about both work and pleasure times. They are both important for your body, as your body needs to rest and work. We must not overwork or underwork ourselves. Remember God also, when he was creating both heaven and earth, worked and rested. There is nothing bad about working hard and there is nothing bad about enjoying ourselves during our pleasure times. Keywords: they must be balanced. It is called work-life balance. More importantly, your work or pleasure times must not keep you away from God as they are both carnal. Everything in this world will pass away and we must not focus on it too much to substitute our presence with God. You must always remember that God created the eternal world but due to human rebellion against God, sin and death entered the world. We must keep our eyes on what we do lest we sin against God. The important thing we must observe no matter what we do is God's "Sabbath," Saturday for our rest. We must not, if possible, do anything on this day if we want to be friends of God. It is upon recognising God in what we do that the concept of eternity delivers us from this conundrum of work versus pleasure. The concept of eternity rescues us from assigning value to all that we do lest it becomes the God we worship. It is imperative to understand that we are not the controllers of our own work lives as Christians. God is in control of our opportunities, locations, and more importantly our gifts and we must acknowledge him and seek his will in whatever situation we find ourselves. It is only when we acknowledge him, and seek his will in whatever we do, that we can excel in life.

## Putting Our Attention on the Invisible Things

Certainly, as Christians, we must put our focus on two perspectives at the workplace in our lives as we are created with two visions. We have the physical vision that enables us to see things in the world that God has created for us, and the capability of vision of our hearts that plan for the physical things to manifest. St. Paul said that we as Christians must look at the invisible things, for visible things were made of the invisible things. If you are a Christian who wants to succeed in the natural world, you must focus your attention on the invisible world. St. Paul here is speaking about the things that are real but not seen. Hence as a Christian, you must seek God's presence in your life in the form of his love, glory, peace, joy, grace, and truth to excel in your work. When you see these things in your life you must acknowledge them and live by them. In the middle of everything we do, we must see God there; if we need promotion at the workplace, in disappointment in life, in the middle of confusion and in the middle of despair of life we must pray for his wisdom, power and understanding to deliver us from the hopeless situations. We must remember that he is for us whether we are in good or bad times.

We must as well understand that everything in the physical world will pass away and we must be cautious in battling it out for the physical things every time. For if our physical eyes are focused on things that will pass away then we will lose the invisible things that are eternal. For instance, at our workplace, we must not focus on the physical location, payment, situation, relationships, position, but focus on the unseen such as God's grace which gives us the consciousness of what we always do because of God's presence with us. The way we respond to everything must be determined by the fact that God is with us and thus his will must be what we first seek before our actions. When we have our place in God's kingdom, we must work consciously according to the way he called us to live. We work thinking of his presence in the form of his power and glory being present with us. It is by doing so that our unseen spiritual reality dictates the physical world reality of how we respond to good and bad moments of our lives. We must be cautious of our present moments that will pass away, and they should not determine our eternal inheritance. *"While we do not look at the things which are seen, but at the things which are not seen. For the things which are seen are temporary, but the things which are not seen are eternal"* **(2 Corinthians 4:18). NKJV.**

# CHAPTER 4:

## BODY AS THE HEALTHY YOU

### Food We Eat

Did you know that what you eat is what will sustain you for a long life here on earth? So, what you eat is what you become, in other words. Your body will respond to what you feed it with. Whether you want to be fat or to be slim depends on what you eat. Our thought patterns, our brain health and our digestive systems depend on what we eat. When we eat wrongly, we become sick and we lose our focus including our focus on our commitment to God in areas such as praise and worship, fasting, praying, and dancing. That is why God is also interested in what we eat as human beings that is why he gave us all the plants and animals for food. Genesis 1:29-30: *"And God said, 'See, I have given you every herb that yields seed which is on the face of all the earth, and every tree whose fruit yields seed; to you, it shall be for food. Also, to every beast of the earth, to every bird of the air, and to everything that creeps on the earth, in which there is life, I have given every green herb for food"; and it was so"*. But what he cannot do is to put it in your mouth and that is why he has left you with choices to make for yourself on what you eat. The choices we make over the food we eat today can lead to good or bad eating habits. Your body needs to be sustained by the food you eat in order to support both your spirit and your soul. Without a body, the soul and spirit become redundant and useless. What we eat in today's world has become critical especially with the introduction of Genetically Modified Food (GM). In this regard, the sources of our food for consumption are no longer natural plants and animals given to us by God. In effect plants and animals have genes altered through the introduction of pesticides, hormones, antibiotics, and other chemicals. By now this would have rung an alarm bell in your head if you did not know.

So, with this in mind, healthy eating must not be an issue you continue to ignore but as a matter of fact a daily consideration in shopping, cooking, eating and refrigeration for the next day. Healthy eating should be about eating foods that are natural and pure in their God created or given forms. The foods we eat must be in their classifications such as carbohydrates, protein, fruits, vegetables, and fat. If you neglect any food in these classifications, then your body will have problems. The foods in these categories must be freshly produced and eaten within a certain time limit. Hence, this will enable you to eliminate processed food items such as flour, salt, sugar, sweeteners, and frozen meat in your diet. We must avoid as much as possible the processed foods and unhealthy ingredients if we are to live a healthy life.

This brings me to the bitter truth that one must face whether to stick with one choice between organic and conventional foods or to stick with both. Organic, being foods produced fresh from the farm, and which grow in rich and organic soil with good nutrients for your body and with no chemicals added. Or conventional foods being food produced from the farm with depleted soil minerals with low nutrients but modified to be produced quickly to supply the market quickly and to a larger extent be kept for long term consumption. The choice is yours, but to me, it must be a little bit of both because we live in a world of scarcity and I do not want to force anybody into the situation where they cannot find what they want and end up avoiding what they need at that particular point in time. But I must say this: try to avoid genetically modified food as much as possible because it is not good for your body. But in an event where you do not have many choices available please take it in moderation. The shocking truth is that conventionally raised cows and chickens have had their bodies pumped with chemicals and hormones throughout their lives making their milk, eggs, and meats dangerous for consumption. So, you must where possible, make the switch to organic meat, milk, and eggs for your consumption. The same should happen with your shopping list of both vegetables and fruits. To avoid chemical pumped fruits and vegetables, you must have the following items on the top of your list: pears, celery, grapes, spinach, strawberries, raspberries, potatoes, peaches, nectarines, bell peppers and apples. The foods that have lower chemical pumped are normally, asparagus, corn, kiwi, pineapple, pears, papaya, mangoes, tomatoes, avocados, cabbage, watermelon, broccoli, eggplant, onions, and bananas. So, it looks like you have a big job to do, but worthwhile.

Let me now bring you to the big elephant in the room, "the Genetically Modified Organism (GMO's). With today's sciences and technology driven by the desire for money, human beings' lives have been put at risk by a few powerful individuals who are controlling the food in industries. There has been an ongoing debate as to what really has human beings become! And many questions are asked along these lines; are human beings having moral responsibility for their fellow human beings? Are human beings really holding on to what are universal morally and ethically accepted values? I am telling you it is no longer God who is not happy with wicked human beings but their other fellow human beings. Let us bring your attention back to what I am about to introduce to you, "GMO's foods". They are animals and plants created through the gene-splicing techniques of biotechnology. It is also called GE or genetic engineering. What this technology does is merges the DNA of different species of plants and animals to create unstable combinations of viral, bacterial, plant and animal genes that are not naturally or traditionally supported in the breeding of animals and plants. So, the food we eat today is no longer natural as it has been tampered with by a few wicked people who are after the money. As much evidence supported by facts suggests, one is able to say that almost 80 per cent of the plants are grown from genetically modified seeds and 80 per cent of animals are raised with genetically modified hormones today in almost all parts of the world. Certainly, it is fair to say that 70 per cent of the foods we eat come from GMO food. It is a fact and if you have doubt, do your own research. So, going into the shopping centre with this consideration in your mind must be a priority to you who will read this book in future. When you go shopping, read the label, and choose GMO-free foods.

Nevertheless, there is also another cause of health problems: "Gluten." It is a protein found in barley, wheat, and rye products, which are in the carbohydrates foods groups. Gluten is used as a thickening agent in soups and sauces as well as in rising and giving the bread a texture. Although it has been in such foods for many years, the problem now is it is eaten in large quantities and frequency in processed foods such as pasta and baked foods more than in the many centuries past.

Perhaps it is used in many gluten-saturated products today than in past years also. The problem of gluten can also be traced to the 1950s where Scientists began to crossbreed wheat to make it shorter, heartier, and easy to grow on the farms. This wheat revolution production has also come with the consequences of too much gluten being consumed by people. The symptoms of being gluten-sensitive are upset stomach, gas, brain fog and bloating, experienced by people who have negative reactions to it. Having known this I would suggest to you that you try to avoid or reduce gluten processed foods such as sauces and baked foods. Furthermore, try to also read labels in the shopping centres to tell you whether the food you are about to buy contains gluten.

Undoubtedly, there is still a small window of opportunity to find organic food in today's shopping centres. There is a list of what are called nutritionists' "superfoods", which provide your body with high minerals, vitamins, polyphenol, and antioxidants. They are as follows; Chia seeds, Gogi Berries, Kale, Flax seeds, and Hemp seeds. I do not agree with completely quitting or avoiding certain foods, as a healthy lifestyle will work better if you are cautious of what you eat. Remember moderation is the word. It does not matter how best we can keep ourselves healthy and fit, God is the ultimate guide of our lives. And as prophet Isaiah says, *"Your ears shall hear a word behind you, saying, "This is the way, walk in it, "Whenever you turn to the right hand or whenever you turn to the left".* (Isaiah 30:21). NKJV.

## Exercises We Do

Exercise is any physical activity that requires a person to move muscles for the body to burn calories. Regular exercise inevitably improves your health in many ways. Whether you are a sporting person or just a normal person who has scheduled regular exercise activity at the gym, you will agree with me that the benefits of exercise are enormous as it improves all aspects of your body's health system from the inside out. The health benefits are namely: increase in metabolism and burning off more calories per day, improvement of blood flow to the brain which helps brain health and memory, the building of muscles and strong bones, strengthening of the cardiovascular system, improvement of blood circulation, increase of muscle flexibility, production of hormones which make us happier and make us sleep better, improvement of skin appearance, lessened risk of chronic disease, improvement in sex drive and help in weight loss, reduced chronic pain, and increase of your energy levels.

The reverse is also true. If we do not exercise, there are body health consequences associated with it. The lack of exercise can lead to the following consequences in people; loss of tissue cell elasticity, risk of chronic disease, build-up of belly fat, daily body fatigue, an increase of type 2 diabetes, obesity and weight gain, loss of muscle mass and function which may result in easy injury, heart disease and even probably early death. The reason why this could happen is that we were created by God as working beings. We were created to till the ground for our food and other personal needs, but in today's world, most of our places of work have been reduced to desk jobs with little or no body movement at all.

Body exercise can also increase the intake of oxygen which in turn will increase our stamina which helps our bodies produce new cells that improve better blood circulation and prevention of many diseases. For instance, one of the body's organs that benefits a lot from regular exercise is the heart. It is an organ that needs exercise more than any other organs of the body. Because when it is at rest it requires less work to pump the blood into your circulatory system. In addition, routine exercises increase high-density lipoprotein (HDL) or good cholesterol and also lower our general cholesterol. The other main beneficiary of our exercise is our physical appearance; how fatter or slimmer we look. The primary cause of obesity is lack of exercise as we take in more calories than we burn, which means we gain weight. Alternatively, when we exercise, we burn more calories leading to weight loss and better metabolism or digestion.

It is important to note that regular exercise is not just an activity but a part of a lifestyle that must be incorporated into your daily to day life. Hence, one of its benefits is that it makes you feel better, and you live longer if you like at the end of the day. The following exercises are important if one is to have better blood and lymph circulation in your body.

Cardiovascular exercise. It is the exercise of the heart. This exercise can just be as simple as walking on the stairs, walking on the street, jumping up and down, running and swimming which can take a few minutes of your time every day. The benefits of this exercise include pouring of oxygen into the cells of your body, strengthening your heart muscles, expanding, and clearing the lungs and building your stamina. Exercises for your lungs and heart are simple to conduct and you should carry them out every day.

**Strength training.** It simply means training your bones and muscles to be stronger for tough times. Your body muscle strength will grow according to the number of training exercises you do every day. You can just start with simple exercises such as push-ups and sit-ups in which you use your own body weight. The more muscles you build the more calories your body can burn to make you feel good and stronger. Additional benefits will include increasing your muscle mass and bone density that helps to reduce osteoporosis. This exercise is about building up stable muscle tone and maintaining it for a very long time.

**Flexibility routines.** Daily stretching and other flexible exercises help reduce tendon stiffness and soreness due to lack of regular movements particularly at workplaces, where people are sitting on the chairs for very long hours. This exercise helps in increasing the function of your joints. It also helps in freeing up congestion in tissues and releasing toxins in your body.

## Sleep We Make

The most important ingredient of living a healthy lifestyle is having a sufficient eight hours sleep. At least this is what is recommended by Doctors for you to recover from your day-to-day routine. To many people sleeping is not an imperative part of their life as they feel that it is more productive to be doing than just sleeping. In today's world, we live a pressurised lifestyle where there is always something else to do or somewhere to be. Sleep deprivation comes in most cases from going to work, doing assignments, reading, shopping, and cooking, watching television, death of family members, drinking coffee and smoking, cold or hot weather conditions and looking after young children if you are parents. It can also be caused by physical illness, mental illness, and ageing. People with health conditions such as cardiovascular problems, stroke, depression, diabetes, and obesity. So, lack of proper sleep can become dangerous when we think that it can take a backseat when life challenges you with packed events and busyness that occupy your sleeping time to solve them.

Certainly, many people do not realise the importance of sleeping time until they begin to experience the symptoms of lack of sleep such as poor concentration, drowsiness, fatigue, body weakness, poor memory, and lack of the ability of your immune system to fight off infections. If these primary symptoms are not quickly addressed it steps up into greater complications such as insomnia, mood swings, depression, hallucinations, and narcolepsy. If these symptoms are not quickly addressed it steps up to increase the chances of heart attack, stroke, and asthma.

The irony is that today many go to sleep and wake up the following morning having not noticed what the body has done during sleeping hours of the night. Hence, sleeping has four stages that one must complete in one night if one is to lead a healthy lifestyle. The stage 1 sleep is the earliest one and the one in which you can easily awaken. At this stage, your brain is able to send out theta waves which are able to clear and calm your mind. The stage 2 sleep= is a moderate or partly deep sleep that we go through every night. At this stage, your heart and vascular system slow down and begin to get complete rest. The stage 3 sleep; This is the deepest sleep which is also called slow-wave sleep. At this stage, our blood pressure begins to drop, and our breathing begins to slow down. This is called muscle and tissue repair sleep. Furthermore, it is also a stage where human growth hormones are released as you are in deep sleep with complete rest and are having your body recharged with energy for the next day. It is important to note that this sleep occurs in the first half of the night. Finally stage 4 sleep. This stage of sleep is also called rapid eye movement (REM). This is the stage where you experience dreams at night. At this stage, your breathing varies as your muscle groups are paralysed which keeps you from acting out the dreams. At this stage also the brain is getting recharged with the energy it needs to function the next day. This sleep according to Dr Philip Gehrman happens in the second half of the night.

Nevertheless, the hormones in our bodies recalibrate during our sleep time. The important organs in our bodies such as brains, nerves and respiratory systems are refreshed and restored during our sleep times. Hormone regulation is another important part of our sleep times. The hunger appetite hormones such as Leptin and Ghrelin both have a role in our body's weight, and they are all regulated by proper sleeping times. Ghrelin is a hormone responsible for the increase of appetite whereas Leptin is a hormone made by fat cells that decrease our appetite. Without a doubt, if these hormones are not regulated properly through proper sleeping patterns, weight loss and weight gain may be too challenging to control our bodies. Get your sleep-in order for better health.

## Some People May Ask; Why is God Interested in my Sleep?

If God were not interested in our sleep then he would not have created day and night. He created a day for your work activities and a night for your sleep. The main reason why God wants us to sleep is for him to communicate with us. God mostly communicates with us when we are in deep sleep at night. It is not a coincidence that scientists and theologians using bible perspectives agree that in the middle of the night right around about a few hours before dawn is where we experience our dreams and visions. In the middle of the night, you are quiet and not distracted by the day's activities and this is a perfect time to hear God clearly either through a voice, vision, and dreams. Similarly, our physical health, morale, and poor concentration can be caused by sleep deprivation. It is so prevalent, most people's mental health problems started with inadequate sleep. **"And it came to pass at that time, while**

*Eli was lying down in his place, and when his eyes had begun to grow so dim that he could not see, and before the lamp of God went out in the tabernacle of the Lord where the ark of God was, and while Samuel was lying down, that the Lord called Samuel. And he answered, 'Here I am!'" (1 Samuel 3:2-4). NKJV.*

# Human Skin

Human skin is one of the important organs of our body that needs special attention. That is why I consider it as one of the areas of discussion under the topic "healthy you". Many people underestimate or altogether ignore the importance of their skin. It is our skin that keeps what we want in and keeps out what we want out of our bodies. Through perspiration, our skin helps remove poisons from our bodies. Furthermore, many people think that respiration of oxygen and nitrogen takes place only in the lungs yet most of it takes place in the skin. For instance, through sweating, toxins are removed from our bodies.

Our skin also benefits from the nutritious foods we eat. We must not undereat or overeat. In most cases where people live with an unbalanced diet, their skin develops toxins and congestion due to the dehydration of their bodies. The skin of a person who depends on an unbalanced diet does not cope very well with the absorption of sunlight, which may cause issues of vitamin D deficiency. Vitamin D is important in one's body to help in the calcium formation for strong bones. When people overeat, it results in diseases such as fatty liver disease, obesity, and type two diabetes, which deprives our bodies of the ability, and particularly our skin, to regulate the right amount of sunlight that goes into our bodies. What God has made for us is good, including our skin, and we must look after it to sustain us here on earth. And in this case, we must have our skin and its functions in mind when we are choosing our diets. A good example in the bible about dieting habits is the case in which Daniel and his friends refused King Nebuchadnezzar's offered menu and instead chose to eat a vegetable diet. This could have perhaps been for other reasons known to them, as the bible has not explained it clearly, but it could have been because of their strict dietary laws (being Jewish rules and regulations), about what they had to eat in the foreign land, or perhaps they saw luxurious food eating in the king's palace would cause them to forget about their God. Any of these may be a possibility. *"Please test your servants for ten days, and let them give us vegetables to eat and water to drink. Then let our appearance be examined before you, and the appearance of the young men who eat the portion of the king's delicacies; and as you see fit, so deal with your servants". So he consented with them in this matter and tested them ten days. And at the end of ten days, their features appeared better and fatter in flesh than all the young men who ate the portion of the king's delicacies. Thus, the steward took away their portion of delicacies and the wine that they were to drink and gave them vegetables"* (Daniel 1:12-16. NKJV).

God's work is evident in everything he has wonderfully made including our skin. Our skin is one of the human body's areas that many people take for granted yet it has an important role in protecting us. For example, it protects us against the sun and regulates the right amount of the sun rays that come to our bodies. But not only that, the multi-layer outer skin protects us from hard objects and surfaces we subject ourselves to when we are doing our daily activities in the outer world. This millimetre of our skin gives us a good mixture of durability, strength and flexibility that enables us to fight the dangers of the outer environment. Today through science, mankind has designed body protective devices that can help us protect our body from the dangers of the outer environment; great indeed, but they are not anything in comparison to our body's skin which is alive and constantly repairing and renewing itself for better protection. Can we not be grateful to our God, for our bodies are wonderfully made by him for our daily lives today.

We must also know that our bodies are not our own as they are the temple of the holy spirit of God. And with this in mind, we must not misuse them. The sad truth today is that we have forgotten the true intention of our bodies including our skin, and we may be mistreating them and subjecting them to harsh situations and conditions due to our own perceptions of them. We have seen black people bleaching their skin because of the perception that black colour is not good in comparison to white colour. We have also seen white people piercing their bodies and putting metallic devices into their bodies and applying tattoos to them affecting the appearance of the skin. For all people who do this, it does not matter whether they are black or white, they have one thing in mind to look better and beautiful. I may be wrong but if this is the case then have we not offended God, who wonderfully made our bodies as king David puts it? Are we not undermining God, that he did not create us wonderfully and beautifully? I must make clear that their truth in these perceptions as it is the works of Satan in his attempt to destroy us.

## Know the True Intention of Your Skin

Skin colour is one of the controversial issues dividing the world today. It has been used by many people who do not look alike, to subject each other to harsh situations and conditions of which one of those is slavery. Resources have been divided and channelled to people according to how they look, even in the same countries. Nations have been ruled according to how people look in the same countries. The rules and regulations of countries have been made targeting and subjecting people who look different to other people into harsh penalties for their mistakes, including even killing them. People who look different to each other have abused, bullied, segregated, discriminated against, killed, and denied opportunities to each other, just because of the skin colour being different. Skin colour is almost certainly one of the main issues of the world today, leading to wars, diseases, and discrimination. But is there any validity to this supported by the bible and science? Let us now look at what the God of the bible and science says about your skin colour.

God created one man (Adam) and one woman (Eve), whom the whole population of the world came from the same skin colour. We also know that after God had destroyed the earth through the flood, he had one man left called Noah, from whom the whole population began again. The whole population of today's earth came from the three sons of Noah, namely Shem, Ham and Japheth. Let me add this possibility to this debate on how today human race colour came about. We know that in the book of Genesis Satanic angels procreate with humans, polluting the DNA of humans. When the violence and crimes had increased on earth because of this, God had to destroy the world through flood and had to save humans through one man – Noah. We know that Noah was born a white man according to the book of Enoch 105. We know that Noah was a son of Lamech. Lamech was a son of Methuselah. Methuselah was a son of Enoch who never died as God took him to heaven alive. Enoch was from the genealogy of the son of Adam called Seth. Because of Noah being white, there is a possibility that among his three sons some of them were black. We could also see this issue of colour with the two sons of Isaac and Rebeca (Esau and Jacob). The two were born with two different colours (Esau being red and Jacob being white). Two different people with two different colours but from the same mother and father. All the secrets belong to God (Deuteronomy 29:29), but whatever reasons he used to create the black, brown, yellow, and white are best known to him. But I am sure of one thing: that intention was good for mankind. God has never created what will divide mankind in the way the skin colour has divided them. God since creation has never said that there is one colour that is better over others so that some might dominate and mistreat the other. God looks at all colours as a wonderful part of his creation and he loves them all. To this effect, there is no reason whatsoever for humans to divide themselves according to the colour of their skins. *"So when her days were fulfilled for her to give birth, indeed there were twins in her womb. And the first came out red. He was like a hairy garment all over; so they called his name Esau. Afterwards, his brother came out, and his hand took hold of Esau's heel; so, his name was called Jacob. Isaac was sixty years old when she bore them"* (Genesis 25:24-26. NKJV).

Science does also support God's position in that skin colour was created among other things to protect and to regulate the right amount of sunlight into our bodies. It has nothing to do with which colour is good and which colour is bad. When it comes to sunburn, there are no black and white. Harsh sunlight could kill if God did not give us skin colours according to the geographical location with regards to exposure to the sun's light. We all know that sun rays are extremely hot and vary according to the geographical location in the world. We must thank God that he has provided us with the skin that has millions of miniature layers of umbrellas, filled with melanin to protect our bodies from the deadly ultraviolet rays that could kill us, irrespective of our skin colour as the human race. It is because of the amount of melanin in people's skin that people appear to have different colours; if the truth be told there is no such thing as black and white human beings. If you take the colours practically and match them to the skins on our bodies, you see the difference in what I am saying. It is scientifically proven that all human beings regardless of race have the same number of melanocytes per square inch. The same thing is also true with albinos according to science; they have melanocytes the same as one of normal human skin colours, but the reason they have white skin is that their granules lack or have affected enzymes necessary for the production of the melanin. Even with the affected melanosomes their stem cells still form umbrellas like normal human skin, but they still have a high risk of sun damage. By the same token, some people have darker skin than others, not because of the huge number of melanocytes but because they retain a great amount of melanin after the skin cells are no longer able to divide, according to science. Alternatively, people with lighter skin colour easily break down most of their melanosomes making them vulnerable to the sun rays. In dark skin colour, the DNA which is no longer vulnerable to UV because the cells are not dividing has some advantages over people of other skin colours. These people with dark skin colour are resistant to cancer and sunburn. But there is also some risk attached to this as these people may have problems with vitamin D if they have little or complete lack of exposure to sun rays. So according to science, there are both advantages and disadvantages of all the colours we have as a human race. So nothing in science supports the human position and perception that there is a better colour of skin over the others. So where did we get these perceptions about the colours of our skin? And the answer is from Satan who wants to divide us and destroy us as human beings.

# CHAPTER 5:

## THE BODY AS A BATTLEGROUND BETWEEN GOOD AND EVIL, TO EACH CARRY OUT THEIR AGENDA

Listen very carefully; all of us (mankind), came from heaven but not all of us (mankind), will go back to heaven. Let me justify this statement. We know that we are tripartite or triune, Spirit, soul, and body. And for each part of us mentioned, God has a plan. Here is the breakdown; Spirit-man (food is the word of God), Soul-man (food is wisdom and understanding), and body-man (foods are natural plants and animals' products). God has designed you and me in a way that all these three parts must depend on him while we are here on earth, on his mission. If you have voluntarily disconnected any of the three parts of you from him, then you have wilfully or un-wilfully joined the devil. Why is this? Because there is no middle ground; you are either with the devil or with God. This is not a strange observation as we have atheists and agnostics who denounce the existence of God. By doing so they have with or without their knowledge voluntarily joined the devil. Yes, someone may argue, but what devil am I worshipping if I have not officially invited Satan to my own affairs? Well, there are other things in your life that you consider more important than God and have taken all your time. This can be your relationship, job, studies, business, power, finances, homes, entertainment, movies, travelling and so forth. I will ask you some questions below to see for yourself exactly whether you are with God or with Satan. Anything that you do without acknowledging the involvement of God is the work of Satan. This may sound like a far-fetched assertion, but it is the truth.

## Do we live to eat, or do we eat to live?
## The answer is: we live to eat

Because the spirit-man was first created before the body-man. Jesus Christ said a man should not live on bread alone but from every word that proceeds out from God's mouth. The food of the spirit-man is the word of God. Our spirits and souls which are God's, feed on the word of God, not our natural food. So, when we eat too much of our natural foods and not enough words of God, we are starving our spirits and souls. The reason why many of us fail to hear from God is that we are not feeding our spirits and souls on his word – the bible. Ultimately also the parable of the rich fool teaches us that; *"The ground of a certain rich man yielded plentifully. And he thought within himself, saying, 'What shall I do since I have no room to store my crops?' So, he said, 'I will do this: I will pull down my barns and build greater, and there I will store all my crops and my goods. And I will say to my soul, "Soul, you have many goods laid up for many years; take your ease; eat, drink, and be merry". But God said to him, 'Fool! Tonight, your soul will be required of you; then whose will those things be which you have provided?' "o is he who lays up treasure for himself and is not rich toward God."* Furthermore, according to the scriptures, God has predestined you and me. God foreknew you and me before we were conceived in our mother's wombs. God said, *"Let us make mankind in our own image."* God is a spirit and he created you and me first as spirits in heaven before he wrapped you into your mother's womb to be conceived as bodies. So, when you and I are born, we are born as spirits in bodies.

Listen very carefully; when you and I were born, God had already finished his work. He had already declared both the beginning and the end of you and me in heaven. That is why everything whether good or bad that happens to you and me here on earth does not come as a surprise to God. *"All things worked together for good to those who love God and those who are chosen for his purpose."* Those things whether good or bad which happen to you and me along our ways are not there to crush us but rather to shape us into our final destination, which is heaven.

Before you and I became bodies, God had already assigned you and me jobs we would come and do on earth. A good example here is the prophet Jeremiah who was given his assignment as a prophet before he even became a body (person). The world called it your passion and God called it your mission on earth. You must stop looking for your assignment from people and seek God for it. He has it for you. Every single person on this planet is not an accident, you have a purpose for which God created you. And you must find your purpose within you. God has already put it in there. Do not look to others, look to yourself. When you have found your purpose within you, you will have value and people will come to you because of your unique gifts. It is important to note that God does not necessarily need every single person to be a preacher of his word, but rather his sons and daughters to fear him and to work in other disciplines which may require his work. God wants to raise politicians, doctors, lawyers, scientists, leaders, and business people who love him and love other fellow human beings.

## What will be your life after this life on earth? The answer is you will go back to God as a spirit and soul, as the body will go back to the ground

God is immortal (deathless), by nature. God has also given us Christians the same immortality as those who believe in him. Luke 20:34-38: *"Jesus answered and said to them, 'The sons of this age marry and are given in marriage. But those who are counted worthy to attain that age, and the resurrection from the dead, neither marry nor are given in marriage; nor can they die anymore, for they are equal to the angels and are sons of God, being sons of the resurrection". But even Moses showed in the burning bush passage that the dead are raised when he called the Lord 'the God of Abraham, the God of Isaac, and the God of Jacob.' "For He is not the God of the dead but the living, for all live to Him."*

God's plan for you demanded surrendering your will to him completely and trusting in him for all your provisions; all things, in all situations, and at all times—in both the good times and the worst of times, in sickness and good health, in prosperity, in war and prison. It is a plan that is full of spiritual warfare yet is all winnable. Because Jesus Christ already won the battle for you on the cross. It is a plan where one learns to fight the good fight of faith. It is a plan of many tears yet great joy when victorious.

God's plan for you demands you surrender your will to him completely, and trust in him for all your provisions, all things, in all situations, at all times, in both good and hard times, in sickness and good health, in prosperity, war and prison. It is a plan that involves spiritual warfare, but it is winnable. Because Jesus Christ has already won the battle for you on the cross. It is a plan where one learns to fight the good fight of faith (1 Tim. 1:18). It is a plan of many tears, yet great joy when victorious.

It is a plan that dates back to the creation; God put within you a seed of greatness. In every single human being, plant, and animal there is a seed of greatness that produces, multiplies, supplies, and subdues. This seed is unique in every human being, plant, and animal. That is why every single human being reproduced offspring that is a resemblance to him/her. Every single plant reproduces the same plant that resembles it through a seed. Every single animal reproduces the same offspring that resembles them. So, this seed of greatness is within you. That is why you must not compete with other people.

But pay attention; Yes, God has a good plan for you, but do you have a good plan for God? I know this question will blow your mind away with the theology you know about God. But that is ok, that is why I am doing what I am doing. God has given you a powerful weapon he cannot take away from you without your permission – (your human will). And this is my simple definition of a human will; your desire to do what you want, including who to believe and worship. When God created mankind, he gave them authority and power to rule the world. If you cannot rule without doing what you desire, then you are a slave, not a leader. If God must intervene in your case, then you must completely surrender your "Will" to him. You must also play your part in receiving a blessing plan for you by God. And this should be your plan for God, if you want a breakthrough in your situation; read the bible like never before, pray like never before, fast like never before, be sincere hearted not holding sins, including forgiving those you hold bitterly in your heart, respect his laws, judgements and commandments and I guarantee you, you will see the God of heaven working mightily over your case. You must learn to fight back against the devil. You are at war, do not take it lightly.

This seed can be corrupted by the devil and you must protect it at all costs if you are to prosper and be successful. The devil can corrupt your seed through jealousy, hatred, greed, envy, violence and anger towards God and other people. Once he has done this then has taken over your will and he will begin to direct and dictate what you do. If you begin to hear things like these within you, you will never succeed, you will never have a peaceful marriage, you will commit suicide, you will never have properties, you will never recover from sickness and so much more, then you know that the devil has taken over your will. You know that it is no longer you and God who controls your will, but the devil. Once you are going through these then it is time to seek a solution to your problems. Do not be deceived; no devil will cast out the devil. It is only God who can cast out demons. Seek God for all your problems whether small or big. Nothing is difficult for our God. He is the king of the devil. To those who are shattered and broken down by medical reports, please listen to me very carefully; you have no reason to be terrified about it. What the medical doctors do is report well examined and well-tested results about the state of your body at that point in time. It is a facts-based report about you. There is no doubt about that, but you must move beyond science. And here is the justification, who is controlling you? Who has a good plan for you? Who has a bad plan for you? Who has a bad report for you? Who has a good report for you? Once you have answered these questions correctly, then you have moved into the supernatural world, where your next answers will be based on faith and hope in God. Shun all those bad reports about you from the demonic world and turn to the God of heaven; he has a good report about you.

To those in a state of despair, disappointment, and hopelessness about themselves. Let me tell you this; there is nothing wrong that you have done that is different to others, but the devil is attacking you because of your seed of greatness within you. The devil is not a crazy and useless being that goes around attacking everyone all over the place. He is a clever and cunning being who aims a targeted attack against people who could be dangerous to his kingdom. Mark:5 – I will bring to your attention the man in the region of Gadarenes who was possessed by six thousand demons, because of the greatness which was in him. Upon being freed from the demons by Jesus Christ he went and proclaimed the message of the greatness of God's kingdom in his home region of Decapolis, which had ten cities. That is how great you can be. The good news is that you still have your will which cannot be touched by God or the devil. You can choose to stay in your problem, or you can choose to be out of your problem by seeking God wholeheartedly. You still have a life to live here on earth. Your mission is not over so long as you are alive.

## This is How Satan Wants to Control Your Body

Satan can get humans to work with him or influence them in the following ways or more: He can get you to believe his lie (that there no God), purposely to steal, to kill and destroy your soul in hell; Satan, with all power, signs, and lying wonders, and with all unrighteous deception can mislead many people who will eventually be burned in hell with him, by God. Satan, as you are busy doing other things for life, is accusing you in heaven, to take custodianship of you and your children (generational inheritance). Satan is generational as God. He still has access to heaven today, but have you asked yourself; What is it for? Satan knows who among the Christians is being used by God and who has the holy spirit of God-that is the one he goes and report whenever he has sinned. *"And the evil spirit answered and said, 'Jesus I know, and Paul I know; but who are you?' Then the man in whom the evil spirit leapt on them, overpowered them, and prevailed against them so that they fled out of that house naked and wounded."* Satan once cast out through, for example, baptism in a believer can return to the believer, if the believer is not a committed Christian thereafter. To make matters worse he goes and gets himself seven more wicked demons to make your condition worse than the last one. Satan can distort God's intentions for marriage. The behaviours we see today in same-sex couples (men with men and women with women), is the same behaviour we saw in the men of Sodom and Gomorrah. Satan can get you to curse yourself and others by speaking bad words against yourself and others. *"From within, out of the heart of men, proceed evil thoughts, adulteries, fornications, murders, thefts, covetousness, wickedness, deceit, lewdness, an evil eye, blasphemy, pride, foolishness."* Satan can influence your imagination and thoughts to sin against God. Satan can block believers' prayers. If they stop praying, God can never answer their prayers. If he can block Daniel's prayers (a true friend of God) then who do, we think we are? Satan cannot operate without a body, and if he cannot get the human body then he can use other living things bodies (animals).

## Can Demons Possess Believers?

The answer is no. But watch this carefully; the only Christian a devil cannot possess is the one who applies the word of God, blood, and name of Jesus, sticks to the truth, accepts the holy spirit, fasts, and prays continually. The rest are already captives and prey or can be prey and captives of Satan in the foreseeable future. The Devil is real, and he is obsessed with the destruction of your (finances, marriage, sicknesses, vision, and mission). He has amassed knowledge over years in dealing with mankind on earth, and he is wise, cunning, subtle, and deceptive to human beings. He has existed and will continue to exist, even after we have died. Spirits do not die. That is a fact.

Mankind is tripartitely made up of body, spirit, and soul. The human being is a spirit that has a soul which lives in the body. When believers are saved their spirits are alive again in Christ. Jesus said in John 3:5 that we must be born again of the spirit. God (who is a spirit) communicates with us through our spirit. Demons cannot dwell in our spirits as our spirit is the residence of the holy spirit of God. And where the spirit of God is, there is liberty (2 Corinthians 3:17). The apostle Paul put it crystal clear here 1 Thessalonians 5:23 – "***Now may the God of peace Himself sanctify you completely; and may your whole spirit, soul, and body be preserved blameless at the coming of our Lord Jesus Christ.***" When we are saved our spirits, souls and bodies are taken over completely by the holy spirit of God. Hence the devil cannot dare touch us.

That does not mean Satan has no access to the believer. He cannot possess the spirit, soul and body but he can attack them indirectly. Satan can attack us through fear, doubt and worry from the sins we refuse to repent of, grudges we hold against other people and disobedience to the will of God in our lives. He can also cause sickness, family divorce, financial difficulty, depression, confusion, anger, and childlessness for believers who are ignorant about his devices (weapons). The apostle Paul said, we must not be ignorant of the devil's devices lest he gains an advantage over us (Christians).

## Can Demons Read People's Minds?

The answer is no. The bible is clear on this argument: ***"Then hear in heaven Your dwelling place, and forgive, and act, and give to every one according to all his ways, whose heart You know (for You alone know the hearts of all the sons of men)"*** 1 Kings 8:39. If Satan read people's minds he would have not crucified Christ who had the ultimate plan to save mankind from the devil, by his death on the cross and his resurrection. It is only God's absolute power to read people's minds. Satan cannot read your mind, but he can influence it through suggestions to you. For example, if you are angry with someone and you fight them, you are always presented with two choices: good (peace) or bad (war). If you take peace then you have taken God, and if you take war you have taken the devil. That is a simple narrative of a big picture.

Demons can also accurately predict what is inside your mind through mood, tone of voice, words, and complete demeanour just as your thoughts can be influenced by the books you read from other authors and foods you eat with different tastes. Once they have successfully influenced you, they are now able to disconnect your spirit, soul, and body from Christ, and you will be destined for destruction (hell). It is important to note that it is not the devil who makes your disconnection from God, but you as a person. Your will (desire), which God has given you is under no condition; a devil or God will take it away from you.

That is why if you surrender your will to God you will be saved, but if you surrender it to the devil you will be burned in hell. That is what Adam did, he surrendered his will to the devil in the garden of Eden. And was subjected to harsh penalties by God.

## Can Demons See People's Future?

The answer is yes but with less or little accuracy which can sometimes turn out to be true or false. Satan uses the spirit of divination and fortune-telling to predict people's future according to the bible. This is dependent on the power of the spirit behind it. They gather data, facts, information, indicators, and conditions about people to predict people's future. Acts 16:16-24 – *"Now it happened, as we went to prayer, that a certain slave girl possessed with a spirit of divination met us, who brought her masters much profit by fortune-telling. This girl followed Paul and us, and cried out, saying, "These men are the servants of the Highest God, who proclaim to us the way of salvation." And this she did for many days. But Paul, greatly annoyed, turned and said to the spirit, "I command you in the name of Jesus Christ to come out of her." And he came out that very hour. But when her masters saw that their hope of profit was gone, they seized Paul and Silas and dragged them into the marketplace to the authorities. And they brought them to the magistrates, and said, "These men, being Jews, exceedingly trouble our city; "and they teach customs which are not lawful for us, being Romans, to receive or observe. "Then the multitude rose up together against them; the magistrates tore off their clothes and commanded them to be beaten with rods. And when they had laid many stripes on them, they threw them into prison, commanding the jailer to keep them securely. Having received* such a charge, he put them into the inner prison and fastened their feet in the stocks."

But despite this, they cannot absolutely predict people's future. Only God the creator can make predictions of his creatures correctly and accurately. As he has already predestined them (mankind). God can also declare the end from the beginning, making him the master of certainty. Isaiah 46:9-10 **says,** *"Remember the former things of old, thing so fold, For I am God, and there is no other; I am God, and there is none like Me, declaring the end from the beginning, and from ancient times things that are not yet done, saying, 'My counsel shall stand, and I will do all My pleasure".*

## Can Demons be Omnipresent?

The answer is no. Satan is a fallen angel and he has no absolute power, only God has. Demons dwell in either humans or animals' bodies. As Jesus Christ did, once they are cast out from one body they go to another body. So, they cannot be everywhere at the same time as God. But they wander the earth from one part to the other. Job 1:6-7 **says,** *"Now there was a day when the sons of God came to present themselves before the LORD, and Satan also came among them. And the LORD said to Satan, "From where do you come?" So, Satan answered the LORD and said, "From going to and fro on the earth, and from walking back and forth on it."*

## Can Demons Resist Christians Commands?

The answer is no. No Christian being used by the holy spirit, who reads and uses the words of the bible, fasts and prays, and uses the name and blood of our Lord Christ will be resisted by Satan. Christians must understand that all the powers of our Lord Jesus Christ have been given to us, to cast out demons, and they must obey. Mark 16:15-18 **says,** *"And He said to them, 'Go into all the world and preach the gospel to every creature.' He who believes and is baptized will be saved, but he who does not believe will be condemned. "And these signs will follow those who believe: in My name, they will cast out demons; they will speak with new tongues; "they will take up serpents; and if they drink anything deadly, it will by no means hurt them; they will lay hands on the sick, and they will recover."* Unless a Christian has wilfully disobeyed, sinned, and continues to have grudges against people, demons cannot stand a chance against them. With all of these we have seen, Satan can prevent you from discovering that you are destined for hell. If there is one thing the devil hates the most then it is the soul that works for God and who is destined for heaven. Because he was from heaven and he will never go back to heaven, he can throw everything at you here on earth in order for you to miss your salvation.

# CHAPTER 6:

## BODY IF SAVED WILL BE REUNITED WITH YOUR SPIRIT AND SOUL AFTER THE COMING OF CHRIST

For you to be able to succeed in all areas of your life in this world, if you are a Christian, you need God. Because he is your creator who created you to come and accomplish his specific mission here on earth. His mission, not your mission. I repeat, his mission not your mission. Unless you are right with him, he will never release his mission for you. You can choose to go it alone like many have done already but bear in mind that it will be short-lived as it will be cut short or frustrated by Satan who does not want you to amount to anything. Part of your going back to heaven is attached to your assignment here on earth from God.

## What is God's Will for Your Body?

And here it is: Plan to save your spirit, soul, and body. This plan has two phases; the first phase, your spirit and soul do not die and need to be reconciled back to God now on earth before you die. The spirit of God is here right now on earth looking to reconcile the spirits and souls of those who seek God, back to God. Your Spirit and soul do not need the material things of this world including the food we eat. If you do not believe there is God or whether you are not sure whether there is God, your spirit and soul will be in eternity with the Devil in hell when you die rejecting God. It is for this reason that if you want things of God, your spirit and soul must be first right with God. This is his plan for you that you must believe in the name of his dear son the Lord Jesus Christ, whose blood and flesh must save you from death to life. John 3:16 says, **"For God so loved the world that He gave His only begotten Son, that whoever believes in Him should not perish but have everlasting life."**

That is why Jesus Christ said, in Matthew 4:4, **"But He answered and said, "It is written, 'Man shall not live by bread alone, but by every word that proceeds from the mouth of God.'"** Listen to me very carefully, your spirit and soul do not need food we eat but the word of God. You must accept this fact.

## What is God's Plan for Your Body?

To save it from permanent isolation from him. When you die as a Christian, your body will change form from mortality to immortality in Christ. Let me make clear that the body that will come and rule with Christ for one thousand years will be an immortal body, not your current body. This argument is proven in the transfiguration of Christ. Christ transfigured at the Mt. of Olives in the presence of Simon Peter, John, and James, by putting on a new body (immortal body). But not only that, Moses and Elijah appeared in their immortal bodies to the disciples also proving to us that our bodies can change when we die.

Mark 9:2-4 says, *"Now after six days Jesus took Peter, James, and John, and led them up on a high mountain apart by themselves; and He was transfigured before them. His clothes became shining, exceedingly white, like snow, such as no launderer on earth can whiten them. And Elijah appeared to them with Moses, and they were talking with Jesus.*

The perishable body which is the temple of the human spirit, soul, and the holy spirit of God is the attention of many people on earth, yet they forget to target even their immortal bodies, they will need it when Christ comes back. This is the phase many people focus on a lot, yet it is less important to God because of its perishability. People worry too much about their families, finances, power, and authority to the extent that they forget that they need God for their spirits and souls. This is referred to as works of the flesh that have nothing to do with your spirit and soul which are God's. God knows that you need a job, health, finances, family, power, and authority, which can be added to you in abundance when you first seek him. When you are working hard to please this perishable body you are very far from God, and spirit and soul will perish with the body. When you are working to please your body, know that you are a slave of your body, the result of which is death in hell. If you are focusing too much on the below work of the flesh, then know that you are destined for hell. Nothing shall save your body from all these things.

Galatians 5:19-21 **says,** *"Now the works of the flesh are evident, which are: adultery, fornication, uncleanness, lewdness, idolatry, sorcery, hatred, contentions, jealousies, outbursts of wrath, selfish ambitions, dissensions, heresies, envy, murders, drunkenness, revelries, and the like; of which I tell you beforehand, just as I also told you in time past, that those who practice such things will not inherit the kingdom of God".*

Luke 12:16-20 **says,** *"Then He spoke a parable to them, saying: 'The ground of a certain rich man yielded plentifully. And he thought within himself, saying, 'What shall I do since I have no room to store my crops?' So, he said, 'I will do this: I will pull down my barns and build greater, and there I will store all my crops and my goods. And I will say to my soul, "Soul, you have many goods laid up for many years; take your ease; eat, drink, and be merry."' But God said to him, 'Fool! Tonight, your soul will be required of you; then whose will those things be which you have provided?'"*

When a person dies, he receives a different body, called an immortal body. The reason we die is that our current bodies are under the curses of Adam. Our current bodies are broken down quickly by the desires of the flesh which continue to let us commit sins against God. Hence bringing death to us. When we die but are saved by God, our bodies will be given immortality (the body that will never die or decompose). The body God gives will be spiritual, not a natural body. It will be an incorruptible body or immortal body. The reason why it will be immortal is that it will be free of sins that kill our natural bodies. It is a building and house from heaven. It will be a body made by God and eternal in heaven. Just immediately after we die our bodies, if we are saved, will inherit immortality just as the bodies of Jesus, Moses and Elijah. So, you need to work hard for your next body after death, which will be immortal. Just as you work hard for your spirit and soul to be saved you must also work for your body to be saved so it can change forms when you die.

1 Corinthians 15:44-49 **says,** *"It is sown a natural body, it is raised a spiritual body. There is a natural body, and there is a spiritual body. And so it is written, "The first man Adam became a living being." The last Adam became a life-giving spirit. However, the spiritual is not first, but the natural, and afterwards the spiritual. The first man was of the earth, made of dust; the second Man is the Lord from heaven. As was the man of dust, so also are those who are made of dust; and as is the heavenly Man, so also are those who are heavenly. And as we have borne the image of the man of dust, we shall also bear the image of the heavenly Man.*

In short, according to this book of Corinthians 15, Paul mentioned five changes that will take place in our bodies immediately when we die, and saved, or when Christ returns: mortal to immortal, humiliation to glory, corruptible to incorruptible, weakness to power and natural to spiritual. All these curses came on us as the result of the Adamic curses. The importance of coming to Christ is to get rid of these curses among other things that may be generational as well. So long as we are in these bodies, we will continue to experience the effects of the curses in abundance or avoidance at times. Nonetheless, we must learn to endure them all, in both the bad and good times because Christ is our strength.

St. Paul made it very clear, also in the book of Philippians 3:20-21 that our citizenship is not on earth but in heaven where we will put on different bodies. Those who die in Christ now immediately put on different bodies as they head to heaven.

Philippians 3:20-21 **says,** *"For our citizenship is in heaven, from which we also eagerly wait for the Saviour, the Lord Jesus Christ,* *who will transform our lowly body that it may be conformed to His glorious body, according to the working by which He is able even to subdue all things to Himself"*.

Paul here divided our bodies into lowly and glorious bodies. The one we have now, and the one we will have immediately after death heading to heaven if we are saved. In short, we have our current bodies as the bodies of curse and our next bodies will be the bodies of glory as Christ has redeemed us from the curses of Adam and the curses of law under Moses.

The current bodies we have are the bodies of humiliation because of the curses of Adam and Eve. The moment we are born, our current bodies are subject to death after hundred twenty (120) years, confined to movement, breaks through wrinkles, and decay after we die.

# PART II:

## SOUL, THE ENGINE OF HUMAN OPERATION

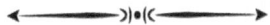

I refer to the human soul as mankind's engine of operation because it is the centre of the decision-making process which enables us to take a positive or negative line in how we think, speak and act. That is why it is the target of God and Satan. The human soul is the area in which human beings can reject both God and Satan. It is the centre of your decision-making process that influences your entire life. Whether it is for good or bad, your decisions are made in your soul. The soul is the composition of your intellect, your mind, and your emotions. The soul is the bridge between the supernatural world and the natural world. The natural world, in which Satan is the master, operates through your five senses such as your sight, taste, smell, touch and hearing. The supernatural (God) world operates through your spirit. But I will not talk much about God because he has no intention to destroy you but rather about Satan and how he accesses your brain to control your thoughts in

# HUMAN BEING AS TRIPARTITE; BODY, SOUL & SPIRIT

## THE MANIFESTATION OF A PERSON WHO CONTINUES TO LIVE BY FLESH AND NOT BY THE SPIRIT

### LIVING ACCORDING TO THE FLESH
1 Corinthians 3:3 carnal 'Christians' behaving like mere men; 3:16 "Do you not know that you are the temple of God and that the Spirit of God dwells in you?"

**FLESH** (Rom. 8:8)
The ingrained habit patterns still appeal to the mind to live independent of God.

*a human mind and the mind of the spirit*

**MIND**
Double-minded

**SPIRIT**
(Rom. 8:9)
Alive but quenched
(1 Thess. 5:19)

*the born again person has a spirit born of the Holy Spirit*

**BODY**
Tension or migraine headaches, nervous stomach, hives, skin rashes, allergies, asthma, some arthritis, spastic colon, heart palpitations, respiratory ailments, etc.

**EMOTIONS**
Unstable

*driven by the natural man – the old unregenerated man*

*but the sons of God are led by the Holy Spirit*

walk after the flesh (often)

*Fruits of the flesh; flesh and blood cannot enter the kingdom of God*

immorality      outbursts of
impurity              anger
sensuality       disputes
idolatry           dissensions
sorcery           factions
enmities          envying
strife               drunkenness
jealousy          carousing

walk after the Spirit (seldom)

*Fruits of the Spirit*

love
joy
peace
patience
kindness
goodness
faithfulness
gentleness
self-control

*https://citizenheaven.wordpress.com*

order to destroy you. I will give you the tools you need to understand how the Satanic kingdom can attempt to speak to you and how he tries to control you by influencing the decision-making process that may seem normal to you, in order to not resist him. Someone may ask, how does the devil access my mind to influence my thoughts?

Surprisingly to many people the devil accesses your thoughts through your brainwaves. These brain waves are divided into four namely, alpha, beta, theta and delta. Each of these brain waves functions in the physiological part of your mind. These brain waves are necessary for the understanding of our thought pattern in our minds. Here I will talk about three types of waves excluding the delta wave, which is responsible for our dreams but will not be part of our discussion, but a subject for next time. The three brainwaves coordinate images and thoughts in our minds and how we can process them into data and information that we apply to our daily lives activities. These brain waves are important in our compositeness, our personality, and our deductive reasoning for our existence as mankind.

Between your body and soul are beta brainwaves, which bring information from the outside environment through your five senses into your soul for the decision-making process. Your soul which is your decision-making mechanism has a responsibility to accept or reject the new information. As you are receiving new information through your five senses your beta brain waves are activated to let your brain pick up images of sound, sight, and pictures into your soul through an electrochemical process. Beta brainwaves work in short-term memory processes taking snapshots of pictures of what is happening in the external environment. This process later programs your soul in terms of your decision-making process. In the process, you begin to make decisions that are guided by good or evil in mind. Sometimes you will find it very difficult to make decisions based on the information you have internally with you, that is good or bad. In the battle of your life between good and evil, the spirit world would inculcate into the knowledge of good and evil that would make it difficult for you to make decisions. The Satanic kingdom would have taught you to fear, doubt, and unbelief that are contrary to God's will, influencing through the informed decision-making that you believe are parts of yourself. For example, if the devil has inculcated fear into your mind through previous bad experiences of failure, it is most likely that fear will rule and dictate your future thoughts in the same way. I want you to know that the devil wants you to strive in sin, for sin to become part of your personality as opposed to God's laws.

Between your soul and spirit are theta brainwaves that communicate information from your soul to your spirit. The theta waves are responsible for the fresh information from God to us if we are born-again Christians. That is why God warned us to be cautious of what comes out of our spirits. It brings information in the form of thoughts, pictures, and impressions that the soul receives from the spirit for the decision-making process, and once it is done the soul allows it back to the spirit or the soul must dismiss it altogether. The theta brainwaves are about four and a half beats per second, and they activate a pathway between your spirit and soul enabling the evil spirit to have access or tap into them, making thoughts in your minds. It is because the theta brainwaves that allow your conscience (spirit) to speak back to you when you are about to make important independent decisions for your life. It is also the theta brainwaves that enable the holy spirit to speak to you either by bringing deep revelations of things of God to you or to convict you of your sins when you are tempted by the demonic spirits. It is through theta that your soul knows everything the spirit does and (vice versa), your spirit knows all your soul does. The serpent knew this, that is why he had to use a snake that has a physiological body to communicate with Adam and Eve using theta, leaving thoughts and impressions in your minds.

More importantly, Alpha brain waves are important in your learning process giving you the ability to have cognitive and deductive reasoning. Your soul is taught through external and internal sources from childhood to adulthood using Alpha brainwaves. These brain waves are trained to enable us to think negatively or positively. What we take into us comes from these brain waves. We have been taught by our families to relate to each other in both negative and positive ways. In the same way, God or Satan can train our brain waves in positive or negative ways using our internal and external environment. Satan wants to train your brain to think negatively through some of your past failures to accept failure as part of your human nature that is not from him. Because he strives in sins, so he wants to train you in the same knowledge of sins and laws of sin. For example, Adam and Eve ate the fruit of the knowledge of good and evil and they discovered that they were naked, yet they had been naked all along since they were created by God. Every piece of information Satan brings to your mind is to undermine you and your relationship with God. The majority of people today find it difficult to hear God's voice not because God is not speaking to them, but because Satan has made it difficult to believe that God can speak to mankind.

Through the Alpha process, God wants to train us in the knowledge of him. He wants us to have a one-on-one relationship with him. Therefore, the bible says that our mind must be renewed or armed with the mind of Christ to think beyond the knowledge of sin and the law of sin. God wants to train us in the knowledge of himself through the holy spirit to know him as a source of truth and good. It is by so doing that your personality and your soul becomes composites of your identification. From the knowledge of good and evil mankind's character was poisoned by the deception in the garden of Eden and God wants to correct this within us. When God created human beings, he created a good being with no evil nature in him. From this argument, it must be made crystal clear that your decision is not always yours. You have become part of what was not originally part of you. That is why when you are in Christ, God wants to remove the sinful nature in us by sanctifying our spirit, soul, and body to be compatible with his spirit. Now once that is done you are sanctified; your human nature becomes what God intended originally before the fall of mankind through Adam. When this happens, you can now make your decisions by being cautious of their negative and positive consequences in your life and that of others.

# CHAPTER 7:

## WILL (DESIRES)

## Human Will!!!

What is it? Where did it come from? What does it do? Human will is the ability for mankind to do what they want without involving God. It is simply doing the desires of our hearts without interference from external forces including God.

***"For I know the plans I have for you," declares the Lord, "plans to prosper you and not to harm you, plans to give you hope and a future.** Jeremiah 29:11."* NIV

According to this verse, humans come from God. What is interesting today is the fact that people of the world have rejected God and have chosen to go it alone with their desires for their future without God. What they forget is the fact that God has blessed them with great ideas in their minds to have a better future, yet they have rejected God. Many people have gone off track in their vision and mission for their lives because they have brushed off God and go it alone into the future, they do not know themselves. When people fail in their "will" they begin to be confused and lose direction. Some will begin to blame God afterwards, the God they never consulted in the first place for their "will." Human will according to the philosophical definition, is a decision-making process of mind that selects a desire among the various desires present. Within philosophy, the human will is important as one of the parts of the mind, along with reason and understanding that make a human being complete with the course of action to pursue his or her life. According to the world perspective, it comes from human beings themselves. But that is the world view of human will but let us look at the human will from God's perspective.

This is exactly what happened to the Israelites who were in exile in Babylon. They had abandoned God in Babylon and followed the ways of Babylonians; intermarrying with them, worshipping their gods and idols, and most importantly not settling down for the seventy years God said they would be in exile in Babylon. There within them rose many prophets who proclaimed to them that God would quickly return them to the land of Israel. When all the plans about their future remained unfulfilled as years went by without returning to Israel, they become confused and hopeless about their future. The word of God came to them through the true prophet of God Jeremiah, that they must settle in Babylon, giving their sons and their daughters in marriage, establishing their own businesses, building their houses, and cultivating their land for food and until the seventy years were over. This was the true God plan for them.

There is delusional thinking today around the world that God of the Universe voluntarily cares about people. This is not true; it must be corrected. Yes, God has a good plan for you as your creator, but you must seek him for it to come to pass. The book of James has put it clearly:

*"What causes fights and quarrels among you? Don't they come from your desires that battle within you? You desire but do not have, so you kill. You covet but you cannot get what you want, so you quarrel and fight. You do not have because you do not ask God."* James 4: 1-2.NIV.

The major causes of war around the world today are the desires of our hearts that remain unfulfilled because of our rejection of God almighty who has a plan for every single person born into this world. Many people have done wrong things and follow wrong plans that are not from God. Because they have refused to ask God for their plan. They think they have God's blessings when they have succeeded in areas such as education, job, house, marriage, power, business, and any other luxurious things of this world. But this is not true God blessings, and God's plan for your life is much better and greater than all these combined.

The scriptures tell us that God has a perfect and pleasing plan or will for your life and here is how you can know it. *"Do not conform to the pattern of this world but be transformed by the renewing of your mind. Then you will be able to test and approve what God's will is—his good, pleasing and perfect will."* (Romans 12:2. NIV).

By the renewal of your mind, you will align your thinking with the thinking of God almighty. It is by doing so that you will become a magnificent person in the image and character of Jesus Christ. And I can assure you that nothing can stop you from becoming like Jesus Christ. The following verses in the bible talk about the kind of person we become when we arm ourselves with the mindset of Jesus Christ.

**Colossians 1:9-10.** *"For this reason, we also, since the day we heard it, do not cease to pray for you, and to ask that you may be filled with the knowledge of His will in all wisdom and that you may* *walk worthy of the Lord, fully pleasing Him, being fruitful in every good work and increasing in the knowledge of God."*

**Ephesians 5:15,17.** *"Be very careful, then, how you live – not as unwise but as wise---Do not be foolish but understand what the will of the Lord will be."*

**1 Peter 2:5.** *"For this is the will of God, that by doing good you should put to silence the ignorance of foolish people."*

**1 Thessalonians 5:18.** *"Rejoice always, pray continually, give thanks in all circumstances; this is God's will for you in Christ Jesus."*

God's will for us also means our character formation and transformation into the one God needs of us. It means that we must learn to look at life in God's way, not our way. With God being present in our lives we no longer need to operate in fear, unbelief, doubt and unforgiveness in this life. We are no longer limited by failures and weakness, as heaven is in us. The fear of failure and all the circumstances surrounding our lives are brought under our feet. Because he knows our weaknesses, God wants us to grow up in areas of our lives with his full assurances that he is in full control. Fear does not say, the lord, I will be with you until the end time. He wants you to be a person who controls situations, not a person being controlled by situations. By this, you become confident in yourself that God is with you as you begin to exhibit excellent character, divine love, and wholesome liveliness.

God's will for our life means also that we must be the masters of our destinies that is reflective of his will for us. This means that we must be able to make our decisions and exercise initiatives and creativity and that we must take full responsibility for them. In the book of Genesis God created mankind in his own image and gave him dominion over all the living and nonliving things on earth to control and to direct through them through decision-making processes that are reflective of

God's will. So, he wants us to have a will in making decisions, but they must be in line with his overall intention for us.

In contrast, God may also have specific assignments for you. If this is the case, then God makes it abundantly clear either through his prophets, vision and dreams, voice, words of knowledge and his bible. For example, St Paul was told to preach to Gentiles, Moses to confront Pharaoh to let the people of God go from Egypt, and Jonah to take the message of repentance to the people of Nineveh.

Sometimes it may be difficult or missed altogether exactly what God will do for our lives due to our arrogance, pride, doubt, unbelief, fear, and even rejecting to seek God for our will altogether because we think we are masters of our destinies. St Paul said, **"Do not be conformed to the pattern of this world but be transformed by the renewing of your mind. By doing this we will be able to test and approve what is God will is for our lives"** (Romans 12:2).

When this is happening to you at a very difficult moment of your life where you are about to make an important decision for life, it must be in line with the teaching of Jesus Christ in the bible. That is why reading the bible becomes important as a guide in making important decisions for your life. The important reason why we must become Jesus Christ's students in his teaching is that he had clarity about the will of his father (God) and the goodness of his followers coping with it. In order not to miss God's will for your life, these are important questions you must ask yourself before making the decision: Is the decision matching the statement "it is more blessed to give than to receive?" Upon making this decision may I trust my God, to later not be worried by it? Will this decision affect my neighbour in positive or negative ways which may be against the teaching of Jesus Christ? Does the decision break the established laws, rules, and regulations of the organisation I am party to? And is the decision matching the sexual integrity rules on marriage and lusts outside marriage? By doing this I can assure you will never miss what is God's will for you in the decision you are about to make and those that you will continue to make in life. On top of that, there is also more to this which we will look at that may also help you in your decision-making process where the will of God is not to be clear or vague to you.

The irony today is that people have rejected God who created them, with little knowledge or no knowledge at all that he has something for them. If this is you thinking this way, then I have good news for you: God has your spiritual gift for you. This could be mind-blowing to you. The bible teaches us that every single person on the face of this earth who is created by God has a gift from God. Perhaps to know God's will for your life you must pay attention to your innermost being. You must understand and embrace your uniqueness within you in the form of your passion, thoughts, imagination, and creativity in application to the world around you. Pay attention to your passion (what you love, desire and are willing to do perfectly is your God-given gift for your life). For example, your passion may be about leadership, inspiration, care, administration, hospitality, business ideas, politics, which comes naturally to you or your desire to pursue. Once you have discovered your God-given gift, hit the ground running with it as time may be against you. Without a doubt, at this stage, you would have discovered the greatest treasure and road map for your life that will never fail you or discourage you later in life. Hence, making the decisions that are spiritually aligned to God's will for your life will give you unspeakable joy that will enable you to achieve great things in life.

*"**But the manifestation of the Spirit is given to each one for the profit of all: for to one is given the word of wisdom through the***

*Spirit, to another the word of knowledge through the same Spirit, to another faith by the same Spirit, to another gifts of healings by the same Spirit, to another the working of miracles, to another prophecy, to another discerning of spirits, to another different kinds of tongues, to another the interpretation of tongues. But one and the same Spirit works all these things, distributing to each one individually as He wills" 1 Corinthians 12:7-11.*

Certainly, comes the important stage and the most difficult one upon discovering your God-given gift for your life. Staying put in your God-given gift to grow from victory to victory with help of God. I cannot emphasise this enough. Jesus Christ said, "you cannot grow to anything unless you abide in me." *"Abide in Me, and I in you. As the branch cannot bear fruit of itself, unless it abides in the vine, neither can you, unless you abide in Me. John 15:4.*

There is no way you can stay with God unless you talk to him. This brings the importance of prayer to God into play. Human beings cannot receive from God unless they pray. People cannot talk to God unless they pray. Pray-pray-pray and always continuously pray without ceasing to God. Prayer is the only means that connects you to your lifelines. When you are about to make an important decision for your life, pray to God. When you lack anything in your life pray to God. Your God-given gift will only come to fruition when you see God's guidance along the way as you make important decisions over it. Your decisions must be based on God's wisdom as it allows us to share the burden with God. There is nothing that scares us more than deciding about our life which is based on different choices, when we genuinely choose, there are consequences, and they may stick with us for the rest of our lives. Making difficult choices is the essence of our adulthood. God wants us to learn how to make our choices very well. That is why the bible is the important source of your guidance if prayer takes too long for you on the urgent matters of your life. Great Poet Archibald MacLeish said, what is freedom? Freedom is to choose: the right to create for oneself the alternatives of choice. Without the possibility of choice, a man is not a man but a member, an instrument, a thing. When faced with tough decisions for your life you must seek God's wisdom instead of asking him for his will for you, which may be a complicated process that may take a long time. You must pray quickly and proceed with his wisdom by looking around you at things that you take lightly yet would have been his answers to your desired outcome. Sometimes God's help comes, having caught us off-guard. Look at this example; A woman locked her keys in her car in a rough neighbourhood. She tried using a coat hanger to break into her car, but she could not get to work. Finally, she prayed, "God. Send me somebody to help me". Five minutes later, a rusty old car pulled up. A tattooed, bearded man wearing a biker skull rag walked toward her. She thought, "God, really? Him?" But she was desperate. So, when the man asked if he could help, she said, "Can you break into my car?" He said, "Not a problem". He took the coat hanger and opened the car in a few seconds. She said to him, "You are a very nice man" and gave him a big hug. He said, "I am not a nice man. I just got out of prison today. I served two years for auto theft, and I have only been out a couple of hours". She hugged him again and shouted, "Thank you, God, for sending me a professional!"

Furthermore, you must learn to recognise God's voice. Many people will be surprised that God speaks to them daily yet do not recognise his voice. Those people who have developed close intimacy and friendship with God can hear his voice daily. They talk about this openly to other people. On the other hand, people who have also devoted their time to God yet do not hear his voice may sometimes doubt these claims. All these assertions may have merits of their own, but one thing is certain, that God does speak. However, one thing is common to many people that it is okay to talk to God, but it is not okay for God to talk to us. No one has put this better than the greatest comedian Lily Tomlin who asked, "Why is it that when we talk to God, it is called "prayer," but when God talks to us, it is called, "Schizophrenia?" There is nowhere else this can be proven than in the bible, with the communication between God and Samuel. On one fine night, the young boy Samuel hears his name being called three times and runs to Eli, thinking that it is Eli calling him. So, Eli who had greater spiritual experience tells Samuel to get back to bed, and when he hears the voice again, he should say, "Speak, for your servant is listening." Sometimes, in life, you may need a mentor like the case of Samuel and Eli as you get mature in the things of God. People over the years must learn the skills and abilities needed to hear God's voice correctly. It comes mostly with experience over time. Developing the ability to listen to God's voice also requires consistent obedience over spectacular discernment. One must develop the habit of listening, making time and space for reflection. It means getting away from television screens and other distractions to a place of total silence.

*"That the Lord called Samuel, and he answered, "Here I am!" So he ran to Eli and said, "Here I am, for you called me" and he said, "I did not call; lie down again." And he went and lay down, then the Lord called yet again, "Samuel!" So Samuel arose and went to Eli, and said, "Here I am, for you called me." He answered, "I did not call, my son; lie down again." (Now Samuel did not yet know the Lord, nor was the word of the Lord yet revealed to him.) And the Lord called Samuel again the third time. So, he arose and went to Eli, and said, "Here I am, for you did call me." Then Eli perceived*

*that the Lord had called the boy. Therefore, Eli said to Samuel, "Go, lie down; and it shall be, if he calls you, that you must say, 'Speak, Lord, for your servant hears.'" So Samuel went and lay down in his place. Now the Lord came and stood and called as at other times, "Samuel! Samuel!" and Samuel answered, "Speak, for your servant hears." Then the Lord said to Samuel: "Behold, I will do something in Israel at which both ears of everyone who hears it will tingle."* 1 Samuel 3:4-11.

# Word of Knowledge

According to Greek, the word of Knowledge is gnosis, which means "knowing" (the act) knowledge. In the bible, it is referred to as a spiritual word of knowledge. For example, Paul used the word of knowledge in 1 Corinthians 12:8 when he talks about the gifts of the holy spirit, to one the words of knowledge through the same spirit, and to another the words of wisdom through the same spirit. Paul here is trying to imply that the spirit of God, while in mankind can operate mightily in men and women who have given themselves to God, as he so chooses, giving revelations about the mysteries of God's Kingdom. To the spirit-filled and spirit-led Christians the words of knowledge give a better understanding of revelations to enrich their lives in their work with God. There are many other examples in the bible where the words of knowledge have been used. Elizabeth knew that her cousin Mary was carrying God's son through a revelation of the holy spirit when Mary visited her. Ananias received words of knowledge about St Paul's conversion to Christianity on the road to Damascus and thereafter prayed for him. My most favourite revelation by the holy spirit is when the ordeal of the discussions between Philip and Nathaniel was all revealed to our Lord Jesus Christ.

God has given us different gifts according to his will for us. Because we are unique in many aspects including our DNA, our colour of skin, our hairs, and even our physical look, is the same way God has given us his gifts. The words of knowledge may function in some and it may not function in others. God communicates the words of knowledge to different people using visions and dreams, and revelations into our spirits. Contrastingly it may be also through the natural environment in the form of living and nonliving things where revelations are through what we see, feel, and hear. I once experienced this when I was preaching the word of God. God deposited into my spirit these words; I have come into the world personally (God), my son has come (Jesus Christ), and the holy spirit is here now on earth and now is the time for people to believe in him before he is withdrawn. What a wonderful revelation by the loving God to me. It is this revelation that has shaped and changed my life and my thinking about God plan for me.

God communicates his will to us in the form of words of knowledge he deposits to our hearts telling us about past, present, and future events. This great gift of the Rhema word is to direct or meet our needs. It is one way God reveals his hidden treasures of wisdom and knowledge that we may understand his mystery to the most trusted children. It is aimed at changing people's situations at that time. It is aimed at helping people who are in desperate situations to give them hope. It may sometimes be unpopular to those who do not want their secrets revealed in public, but it is good at teaching them God's mysterious ways of communications.

People's responses to these words of knowledge from pastors may be different; it may be acceptance or rejection depending on the person and his or her relationship with God. I personally had a few of them over years from different men of God. I welcomed them with shocking exclamations of how God had already known me and my situation. One day my wife Rachel and I were attending Good Success church, and the leading pastor there, pastor Rajan, in the middle of his sermon stopped, stood still, and called out my name: "David, the Lord has told me to tell you that your blessing with children is on the way". I could not believe my ears with what I was hearing. But it was welcome news even though I did not want people to know my childless condition. But over the years I have come to appreciate the administration of words of knowledge as a source of my hope that God knows my problems and he will one day fix them. God continues to use me mightily in this area. Sometimes if I have difficulty understanding a verse in the bible, I just ask the holy spirit a simple question such as this; What does this verse mean? He may get back to me immediately or it may take some hours or days to get back to me with the answers.

## Wisdom

Wisdom is defined as the ability to use knowledge and experience to make good decisions and judgments. It is important to underline these two words, knowledge, and experience, as they are different things altogether, but are used collectively when one has wisdom in making informed choices in life. On many occasions, people associate wisdom with age, and I want to tell you point-blank that these people are deadly wrong. Let me unpack it here for you. Knowledge is data, information and facts about certain things or situations, whereas experience is the condition or the situation you have been in that has given you knowledge, skills through feelings, doing and seeing. So, you can have knowledge but lack experience in the thing or situation, and it has nothing to do with age. Yes, to some degree experience may be associated with age but it is dependent upon things one has gone through in life. We understand in the bible that God through his wisdom frames all things together to work perfectly for himself. We also understand in the bible that God has held back wisdom and understanding to give it to those who love him. So, in a nutshell, you must love God to have his wisdom and understanding.

Certainly, a lack of wisdom is a lack of problem-solving skills. There is nowhere else in the bible this can be shown than in the book of Proverbs of King Solomon, who was the greatest wise man who has ever lived on the face of the earth. The book of proverbs is the treasure for those who love to have wisdom in life. Whether at difficult or at good times you must seek wisdom to make the right decisions for your life. Wisdom is a great treasure for those who seek it – in fact, king Solomon puts it above money or other precious stones such as gold, silver, and bronze in terms of their value. The bible puts it very clear that those who seek wisdom can accumulate great wealth. Through wisdom one can learn the principles, ways, skills, and knowledge it takes to prosper in life. Prosperity does not necessarily mean to have wealth alone but rather to succeed in all areas of our lives including physical health and spiritual health.

According to the book of Proverbs 10:21, fools die for lack of wisdom, and Proverbs 12:15 signals or warns people to not circumvent wisdom for shortcuts, "*The way of a fool is right in his own eyes, but he who heeds counsel is wise*". Whether young or old it takes wisdom in the form of humility to seek good advice and guidance in life to make the right decision on a thing or situation. It is a common saying in almost all the traditions that it is possible to walk with the wise to be wise. For if you choose to walk with the fool you will be destroyed. Individual plans are established through human wisdom and are achieved through human wisdom.

"If one lacks wisdom then let him seek it," according to St. James. ***"If any of you lacks wisdom, let him ask of God, who gives to all liberally and without reproach, and it will be given to him".*** According to James, God has the monopoly of wisdom and he only gives it to people as he so chooses. In this context, King Solomon had to ask for wisdom from God and there is no reason why God cannot give wisdom to you if you seek him. The sources of getting wisdom from God includes prayers, reading the bible, community leaders, national leaders, and churches leaders.

However, we must be careful about wisdom and its source because there are other sources of wisdom. Let us face it there is earthly and heavenly wisdom. Earthly wisdom is a man's wisdom that has its origin in the Satanic kingdom, whereas heavenly wisdom is the wisdom of God. St. James spoke of God's wisdom as being pure, peaceable, gentle, merciful, with good fruits and without partiality. Worldly wisdom has its roots in the Satanic kingdom as the ruler of this world. To make this very clear all a man's thoughts, ideas, creativity, imaginations come either from God or Satan. It must be known that if God is not the source of your wisdom, then know that Satan is. For example, it is very hard for a person not to acknowledge God in their work if they find themselves doing great things of wisdom. A good example is King Solomon who asked God for his wisdom and during his reign on earth, he was able to acknowledge God through his life. This is a source of wisdom many Christians must seek to have peace with God and their fellow human beings. It is marked by love, peace, joy, and unity – looking after the needs of each other. Whereas in the earthly wisdom it was very hard for a person to attribute his wisdom to Satan as it may not sit well with the people, he is leading. Many people who found themselves doing great things give themselves credits and glorify themselves for their success. This is what we know as Satanic wisdom because Satan, out of pride, rebels against God. This wisdom is marked by struggle, mistakes, toil, and pain as human beings with the influence of Satan try to oppress mankind. It is a violent source of wisdom that Christians must not associate with.

*"Who is wise and understanding among you? Let him show by good conduct that his works are done in the meekness of wisdom. But if you have bitter envy and self-seeking in your hearts, do not boast and lie against the truth. This wisdom does not descend from above but is earthly, sensual, demonic. For where envy and self-seeking exist, confusion and every evil thing are there. But the wisdom that is from above is first pure, then peaceable, gentle, willing to yield, full of mercy and good fruits, without partiality and hypocrisy. Now the fruit of righteousness is sown in peace by those who make peace."* (James 3:13-18). NKJV.

# CHAPTER 8:

# MIND (THOUGHTS AND IMAGINATIONS)

## How Our Minds Operate

The mind is the important determiner of what we do in life. *As the man thinks, that is who he is.* Unless you understand that what you think determines what you do in life, you will never have an idea of the roles of your mind. The way you think shapes your present assignment and enables you to predict its future outcomes (success). Our minds are complex and complicated nerve systems programmed by God to think, react, and feel the ways that catch us by surprise. Our minds are divided into conscious and subconscious parts. The conscious mind receives all the information into the subconscious mind. The subconscious mind processes and reprograms information and restores it to be later used in life. Below are five ways and habits that shape our minds.

**Our own thoughts and words.** You cannot know your potential until you know the power of your words. Your words are everything about you. What you say is what you can be known for. What you say is what you must do. We know that it was through the power of words of God that the world was established, and the spirit of God was hovering over the water to put them into action. Similarly, people can be known by their words whether good or bad. Words we speak create success or failure in our minds, which later determine the results of what we do in life. As you converse with people you will hear sayings such as "I can do that", or "I cannot do that", "That is possible to do" and "That is impossible to do", and "I will never amount to anything in life". So, we determine our success or failure by our words before our actions. It is easier to think negatively than positively in our minds because we live in a world where we rely too much on what is happening outside us than what is happening inside us. This is dangerous because we are dependent upon the words put into our minds by our parents, friends, teachers, colleagues, politicians, and other successful people in life. If this sounds like you then I have good news for you; your mind must be programmed to God capabilities. Because he is your creator, and everything about you is with him. There is no negativity and failure with God. Now is the time to turn to him.

**Our own five senses and feelings.** We experience and figure out the world around us through our five senses – seeing, smelling, touching, tasting, and hearing. The impressions about ourselves and the people around us are formed out of our senses that become thoughts, pictures, and feelings in our minds. The response to the world around us is shaped and determined by the thoughts in our minds, which in the long-term moulds our characters. This means the environment we expose ourselves to, becomes important. What you involve yourselves in is what you will become in long term. For example, if you associate yourselves with gossipers, adulterers, slanderers, thieves, robbers, you will become one. So, you can see how negativity can be contagious. It is also very important to control what we take in through our senses as it may determine our attitudes, moods, and feelings. As we speak and act based on our feelings and emotions they become deeply embedded in our minds. When what we think is no longer driven by our conscience but our emotions and feelings, then we are in a dangerous situation.

**Our old habits.** Our minds are severely affected by our old ways of doing things. Because of our past sins and transgressions, we committed, our brains keep going back to them, reminding us of shame and guilt associated with them. This becomes our mind's programmed response that launched into us in the form of fear, worry, depression, anger, and doubt that affect our decision-making process. Similarly, some other habits such as alcohol consumption, drug abuse, pornography and violence also affect how our brains function. All these addictions hold our brains captive and need to be broken by giving your life to God.

**The hurts in life.** The most dangerous thing about our minds is carrying our past hurts in life as long as we live on earth. The physical, emotional, and verbal abuses by our parents, teachers, friends, colleagues, and relatives leave long-lasting damage in our lives. Such pain of our bitter past at worst can cause depression, stress, anxiety, and mental illness in our lives if we do not get rid of them quickly. The pains which are stored in our subconscious minds imprisoned people's emotions, mood, attitudes, bodies, and interactions with other people around them. The whole of one's life and self-worth are affected as the person begins to withdraw into himself, become defensive, angry, and abusive. Our past hurts may not be triggered by other people but ourselves, sometimes when we blame ourselves for lack of progress in life despite the personal commitment and hard work toward certain goals in life. It does not matter whether our past hurts are caused by us or other people; accept the fact that life has challenges that overcome us.

The fact that we have failed at some stage does not mean that we cannot move on. You must forgive yourself and other people who have done you wrong and move on. God the Father will forgive you if you forgive other people. Bitterness is never a good thing for your bones and your spirit as it may cause diseases that will kill you prematurely.

**The words of others.** The dangerous thing about us is that we tend to believe what other people say about us rather than what we think about ourselves. Some people are completely dependent on other people whether it is a career we choose, a job we do, people we marry and the opinions we form about many things in life. Even if we are mature enough to make our own decision in life, we tend not to trust ourselves more than others. But this is made better if people are giving you positive words of encouragement and it is worse when they are giving you negative words of discouragement. The harsh words of other people create negative Impressions on us and grow in our hearts to become our new identity in our lives. If this, is you then you must stop it. Never give people words meaning in your life as they may create your new self in the image. The more you give people words meaning the more you no longer live by your true self, values, and integrity.

This is even worse for children who depend on their parents to teach them many things in life. At a young age what their parents teach them and tell them is what they carry through their life. If children are brought up in abusive families, they are most likely later in life to become abusive too. If they are put down with words such as these; "You are a devil, you are stupid, you will never amount to anything", they will grow up in life thinking that their self-worth is the opinions of their parents. The bible tells us, *"Children, obey your parents in the Lord, for this is right". "Honour your father and mother, which is the first commandment with a promise that it may be well with you and you may live long on the earth." "And you, fathers, do not provoke your children to wrath, but bring them up in the training and admonition of the Lord".* **Ephesians 6.**

## How do we Program Our Minds for Good or Bad?

As we have seen above, how our brains work is based on the information we take into our brains. This information can program our minds for good or bad. If we are born-again Christians our brains are programmed for things of God (Spirit), and when we are not born-again Christians our minds are programmed for the things of the world (flesh), and the Devil. As born-again Christians our flesh person will still try to dominate our spirit-man unless we upload our minds and our spirits with the word of God, to dominate our flesh.

When we are born-again Christians, we are a new creation in Christ. Our genealogy shifts from the genealogy of our parents who used to worship Satan to the one of our Lord Jesus Christ, Abraham, Isaac, and Jacob who worship God. We become children of God with one family of believers who believe in God. We are no longer identified as tribes, communities, societies, and various human races of the world who do not believe in God, but we become one child of God from different races, communities, societies bound together by one baptism, one spirit and washed by the blood of Jesus Christ. Now God wants us to be transformed to the image of his dear son and bring our minds in line with our new identity. *"Therefore, if anyone is in Christ, he is a new creation; old things have passed away; behold, all things have become new" (2 Corinthians 5:17) NKJV.*

Excitingly as born-again Christians our spirit-person come back alive again. If our spirit- person is back again alive we can feed on the things of God and particularly his word which enables us to reprogram our minds from things of the flesh or world to the thing of the kingdom. This is the only way we can overcome the negative thinking in our minds which holds us captive to the Devil. As you upload your minds with the word of God, it can reprogram your brain from the things of the world that are in your subconscious mind, stored there for many years. As you put the word of God into your brain it will uproot all the unwanted weeds Satan has sown in there for many years – bad habits, rejection, anger, bitterness, violence, hatred, fear, to heal all untrustworthy emotions within you. As you plant and water the word within you, it grows you from strength to strength giving birth to love, peace, calm, confidence, kindness, and unexperienced joy in your life that you never had before. That is how powerful the word of God is to you. It shifts your strength from what you can do to what God can do through you. So, allow him in. He is just waiting for you to make a move of faith through prayer.

Despite the things mentioned above about how you can train your brain to cope with the things of God, there is still one important thing missing, and that is the onus to do what you want to do with your brain. It is you who chooses what goes into it and how to think it through. This means that when we have put the word of God into our brains, we must meditate on it day and night for it to take root within us. The spirit of God is waiting for you to speak the word so that he can plant it in your life. Your subconscious mind which had things of the past are erased as your new conscious mind now operates on the daily intake of the word of God. This is the reality of what you can become as a new person in Christ. You can no longer choose to think of the bad but good only all the time because it is the right way to operate in Christ. At the times you feel like you are downcast you can transform and renew your minds within the word and with the word. It comes to this; you can choose good or evil. It is by doing this that we can create for ourselves the life God wants us to have or the life Satan wants us to have. It is that simple. No if or but about it.!!! ***For the word of God is living and powerful, and sharper than any two-edged sword, piercing even to the division of soul and spirit, and of joints and marrow, and is a discerner of the thoughts and intents of the heart.* (Hebrews 4:12). NKJV.**

## Hearing God's Voice in Our Mind

Undoubtedly, our minds are the battlefields between God and Satan for dominance and control. God wants to control your mind so that he can control you. This is how God practically works in you. If God must work with you, it is the human soul which can accept or reject into our spirits the things of God from the holy spirit. It is important to note that the human soul is independent of God, and you must be made accountable for your actions by God. If God has to work through you then you must consult with him in every single step of your life. If you do not do that then you are no different from Adam. Here is how it works; we know that within us we have both the knowledge of good and evil because of our sin committed in the garden of Eden by eating of the tree of knowledge of good and evil.

For God to work with us, our good nature must be activated within us. So, the spirit of God (the holy spirit), sits within our human spirit, giving us the ability to receive information from God. Our spirit (human spirit) in return relays the information to our soul, seeking permission to allow us to do what God wants us to do. If the soul permits the spirit to receive the information and keep it within us, then the spirit keeps it. If the soul rejects the information within our spirits, then it is disregarded and rejected by our human spirit. Please note that here you have rejected the information from God, but not only that you have rejected the holy spirit and God. Here you are headed for a disaster (Satan).

God talks to us every day. This statement may be a surprise to some and to some it may not be at all. At some stage, you would have heard God's voice very vividly as you experienced that the thoughts in your mind and the words you speak from your mouth did not come from you. Sometimes many people may be caught off guard by speeches certain people give as they have not been known as great speakers. That aside, if you have not heard from God before then I can tell you with great certainty that you now hear from him. It is simple to hear from God. He gives us information or message in our spirits. Our spirits in turn relay into our minds in the form of thoughts and imaginations that become living and non-living in the physical realm. In this context, for instance, Adam was given a responsibility by God to name every living and non-living thing on this planet.

Revelations come from God's spirit to our spirit and thereafter to our minds. So, our minds become the revelation processing mechanism that translates the things of the spirit into words. But in saying that, we have a responsibility to make our minds make sense of, think on, communicate, and apply the revelations of words to the daily activities in our lives.

What happens in our minds is much better and richer than what happens in our natural world. Our minds are the processing centres of what we speak and do in the natural world. Indeed, our mind is a theatre of shapes, colours, sensations, smells, sounds, multitasking and movement which make it a home of imagination and intelligence. And we must look after it very carefully because that is where our success and failure come from. When God speaks to our spirits, we experience that in our minds in the form of sight, sound, sensing and knowing.

## Our Thoughts Must Match God's Thoughts.

When we become born-again Christians, our thoughts are no longer ours but God's. This means that God knows our thoughts before we even put them into action because they either come from him or Satan. He is the master of our minds, spirits, and bodies. This becomes a reality when we are born again Christians. This is the main problem today in the world as men who are educated tend to own their own thoughts with no or little consideration about where they really come from. When we become Christians, we admit the fact that we are not our own but God's. And what we think comes from God our Father through the works of the holy spirit. For example, the bible tells us that Jesus Christ once told a paralysed man his sins were forgiven, as Scribes were secretly accusing him of blasphemy at the same time in their hearts. **"But Jesus, knowing their thoughts, said, 'Why do you think evil in your hearts?'"** (Matthew 9:4). NKJV.

Once we acknowledge and accept that our thoughts are not from us but God, we can tune in to God's channel of communication in order to think like him. By doing this we allow our spirit- person to be receptive to God's spirit (the Holy Spirit), who brings information to us on a daily basis from the kingdom of God in heaven. What does this really mean, "renewing our minds." It means that we must be receptive and sensitive to the information our spirit person receives from the holy spirit as he relays it into our minds. Jesus Christ had to rely on the holy spirit right from when he was baptised in the holy spirit until he died on the cross. He lived here on earth thinking the thoughts of his father about him. The thoughts of God are better, higher, and wonderful because he is our creator. Furthermore, they are more infinite and purer than our thoughts.

*"For My thoughts are not your thoughts, nor are your ways My ways," says the Lord. "For as the heavens are higher than the earth, so are My ways higher than your ways, and My thoughts than your thoughts* (Isaiah 55:8-9). NKJV.

When your mind is renewed, you will be highly attracted to the things of God, creating excessive desires in your spirit and mind for things of God as they are infinitely continuous and precious. In this case, as you read the word of God (the bible) your revelation and understanding increase as the spirit of God begins to reveal to you the hidden meanings of things of God in his word. But this only happens when we shun our natural minds. You must come to God, for the things of God with empty minds, to learn things of God. You cannot understand things of God using your natural mind, as they are taught by the spirit of God to those who wholeheartedly seek him and find him. God will never teach those who think they are more intelligent than him – those who deny his existence and those who are not sure of his existence.

When you get the word of God into your mind, it begins to take root in your hearts and begins to dominate and take over your flesh, which is your entire life. The Bible becomes the source of your provision in the areas of peaceful family relationships, God's favour, prosperity, finances, and protection for your life. It is only through the bible that you can know God's will for your life if you begin to seek him. It contains all the answers for your problems such as doubt, unbelief, fear, discouragement, depression, failure, inferiority, and suicidal thoughts.

Certainly, when we get the word into our minds, it becomes alive in our actions, deeds, thoughts, and speech. At this stage, the word of God becomes alive and powerful in our speech. So, when we decree and declare things, the begins to happen according to the expected outcome. When we begin to speak the words of God in our mouths, the holy spirit of God will begin to reshape them to reprogram our hearts and minds towards the things of God – indeed deep things. Your wisdom, revelation and understanding of the bible begin to increase mightily.

Likewise, your faith begins to grow as you speak, meditate, and hear the words of God loudly and constantly. Perhaps, this is the easiest and most convenient way of growing your faith and taking it to the next level. The most important word is "meditate" on the word, which means think over it again and again. When you read the verse and think over it again and again, getting it into your spirit, the holy spirit will give you a revelation of the true meaning of the verse or words. When you saturate yourself with the word of God, you begin to focus on what God says about you in his word (the Bible). Undoubtedly, when you reach this stage you no longer care about what your friends, boss, relatives, say about you and your own subconscious mind says about your former habits. From here, you begin to think about how God thinks. *"My son gives attention to my words; incline your ear to my sayings. Do not let them depart from your eyes; keep them amidst your heart. For they are life to those who find them, and health to all their flesh"* (Proverbs 4:20-22). NKJV.

## Hearing Satan's Voice in Our Minds

Undoubtedly, our minds are the battlefields between God and Satan for dominance and control. Satan wants to control your mind to control you. This is how Satan works practically with you. For the devil to work with you, you received his information from demonic sources such as demonic books, demonic leaders, demonic television programs, social media, demonic money and so much more, through your five senses into your body. So, what you hear, see, smell, taste and feel if it is good or bad affects you in your innermost being. What you take into your body using your five senses later determines who you are as it is received into your conscious and into your subconscious mind. For the information to be locked into your spirit, the body consults your soul whether to allow the information it has into your spirit. If the soul accepts it and allows the information, it goes into your spirit activating your devil nature within you. The devil becomes alive and active within you. Every time you want to do something bad your Satanic bad nature will dictate God good nature, forcing you to make bad decisions. Here you are surely destined for hell if you do not repent before you die. I am not ashamed to tell you that when a person dies without Christ, they go to a place called hell. There they stay, being tormented in the flame until the time of the judgment. Thus, we see that those in hell will not be there forever, but only until they are delivered up to the final judgment and are judged according to their works and eventually through into a lake of fire.

To understand this better we must first deal with this question; what is sin? Sin is any immoral acts such as evil thoughts, murder, adultery, fornication, theft, false witness, blasphemy, that cause us to fall short of God's glory. They are divided into those that are within us and those outside us. Those that are within us are categorised as sins stemming from our flesh nature – they are things like jealousy, hatred, violence, envy. These sins are manageable and can be controlled by us if we turn to God. These sins came because of our disobedience to God in the Garden of Eden when our great grandfather Adam ate from the tree of knowledge of good and evil. However, there are those sins which are engineered by the Devil, which he commits on us or he causes us to commit on others – they are things like oppression or bondage, blindness, defeatedness, lameness, muteness, wars, family separation, childlessness, financial ruin, accidents and death. These are all engineered and caused by Satan either on us or he gets us to commit them on others. These are beyond your power to control and that is why you need God in order to eliminate them. So, our real enemy is never ourselves or our fellow human beings, as St Paul said: *Finally, my brethren, be strong in the Lord and in the power of His might. Put on the whole armour of God, that you may be able to stand against the wiles of the devil. For we do not wrestle against flesh and blood, but against principalities, against powers, against the rulers of the darkness of this age, against spiritual hosts of wickedness in the heavenly places. Therefore take up the whole armour of God, that you may be able to withstand in the evil day, and having done all, to stand. Stand therefore, having girded your waist with truth, having put on the breastplate of righteousness, and having shod your feet with the preparation of the gospel of peace; above all, taking the shield of faith with which you will be able to quench all the fiery darts of the wicked one. And take the helmet of salvation, and the sword of the Spirit, which is the word of God; praying always with all prayer and supplication in the Spirit, being watchful to this end with all perseverance and supplication for all the saints.* (Ephesians 6:10-18). NKJV.

Similarly, what gives Satan dominance and control of our lives starts with the thoughts in our minds. Whatever gets out of control in our lives starts with a thought. It is not a secret that you and I have gone through periods of sickening and oppressive thoughts in our minds, like sexual immorality, divorce, stealing, corruption, greed, murder, suicide, and violence. These thoughts are what St Paul referred to as wiles and darts of the devil. Thoughts invade our minds all the time. Sadly, some bad thoughts get into our hearts and begin to dictate what we do. They become the source of what we do whether it is good or evil. For example, an experience from the life of Charles Spurgeon serves as an illustration. Having gone through a prolonged period of blasphemous assaults upon his mind and being near the point of despair, he began questioning even his salvation (after all, how could a true Christian think such thoughts?). He finally confided in an aged godly man who asked him one simple question: "Do you hate these thoughts?" Young Spurgeon replied: "I do." The man replied, "Then they are not yours; … Groan over them, repent of them, and send them on to the devil, the father of them, to whom they belong—for they are not yours."

Satan is a clever spiritual being that plants thoughts into your minds which you can begin to think are your thoughts. For him to control and dominate your thinking he must corrupt it through many devices such as doubt, unbelief, unforgiveness and fear. These are the powerful devices he uses individually on you to dictate what you do. If you have not overcome these devices, then know that you have not overcome Satan. Fear is the main weapon of the devil. And they are all unnecessary fears such as losing a job, family divorce, financial loss, and fear of death aimed at controlling you mentally, emotionally, and physically. The purpose is to get you to think wrongly.

Likewise, Satan knows the power of the words we speak, and he will attempt to control our mind and to thereafter, control our mouth and what we speak. "For the power of life and death is in the tongue." He will get you to focus and think on the negative parts of you and others for you to believe and speak negatively about yourself and others. Next, he gets you to be anxious all the time, by concentrating on the problems of your life, which are aided in your mind, and eventually prison. They become repetitive chains of shackles in your minds that never go away. Of course, many people in this state of mind will never think and speak about their future positively. When you begin to speak like this; "I will never succeed in life", I will never recover from this sickness, I will never find love again, and will never find a good job", know that this is not you speaking but a devil within you and you must reject and disown those words.

Nevertheless, the Devil is also a master of isolation. If things have gone terribly wrong in your life such as divorce, loss of job, financial ruin, sickness, and loss of power he reduces you to the state of introspection. At this state you begin to look inwardly, becoming self-obsessed, and self-pitying, causing pain, stress, depression, and even sometimes suicidal thoughts if not suicide itself. Hence, death becomes inevitable at this stage, which is what the devil wants. *"The thief does not come except to steal, and to kill, and to destroy".* **(John 10:10). NKJV.**

Moreover, Satan will also use his wiles or darts such as self-condemnation, rejection, and unforgiveness to torment you. Your whole life will be affected by the bitterness and hurts against yourself or others. The strongest one is unforgiveness. Unforgiveness is refusing to let go in your heart and mind all the toxic abuses, hate, grudges, shame, bad decisions, and mistakes you have committed against yourself and other people. God wants you to forgive yourself and other people so that when you come to him in prayer, you have an untroubled conscience – guiltless of sins. You must forgive all the people; the ones you have offended and the ones who have offended you. I know it is one of the hardest things to do and particularly to those who have offended you without your provocation. To be honest with you I have struggled with it for a very long time, especially in forgiving those who have offended me without my provocation. So, it is not you alone, but you must forgive if you want to be healthy and receive God's blessings. Before I state why God wants you to forgive, let me say why it is good to forgive for your good health in our natural understanding. Firstly, holding all the toxic hate against someone in your heart breaks your spirit. Which in turn breaks down your flesh and bones. So unforgiveness can cause some of the diseases we have today in our bodies like arthritis and so much more. This is not a made-up story; it is scientifically proven. Secondly, it limits opportunities in sharing knowledge, abilities and skills you would have had with that person had you been in a peaceful relationship, including future opportunities where you might need help from that person. So, in the natural world, we must learn to admit our mistakes and the wrongs we have done to each other - apologise and move on for a better future together. Here is why God wants you to forgive; firstly so that you are also forgiven by him. Remember we are all sinners, and if you do not forgive others, God will never forgive you your sins. Jesus Christ died for us all while we were all sinners including the people you hate. Secondly, he wants no sin to be used against you by Satan in the court of heaven to hinder God's blessing for you. These claims are also backed up in the Lord's prayer; *"Forgive us our sins as we forgive those who have sinned against us".* Listen to me very carefully; God cannot bless a sinful heart. God does not need a single person in hell, and so why waste time holding grudges and hate against people. You must forgive so that you are placed in a better position for God's miracles. *"And whenever you stand praying, if you have anything against anyone, forgive him, that your Father in heaven may also forgive you your trespasses. But if you do not forgive, neither will your Father in heaven forgive your trespasses."* (Mark 11:25-26). NKJV.

Similarly, the most dangerous and deadly weapon Satan can use against us is the lack of knowledge about him, his ways, strategies, and tactics. Jesus Christ described Satan as a thief. We know that thieves operate in secrets to steal. Had your prior knowledge as to when the thief would break into your house to steal, he would never steal. The only way Satan can continue stealing from you is when you do not have knowledge about him. Satan knows very well where your knowledge about him compromises your thought realm (your mind). He attacks your mind to confuse it about your ability to know the knowledge of good and evil. Through your lack of knowledge of him, he will deceive you to get you to rebel against God. Deception and disobedience are paramount in your thoughts, and you must watch out for them. No one experienced this more than Jesus Christ at the Garden of Gethsemane when he was troubled in the spirit. He said, *"Not my will but your will be done"*. He knew the terrible suffering which was ahead of him and he was faced with the temptation to avoid it. But he had to look beyond the cross to go through it for you and me. *"But **I fear, lest somehow, as the serpent deceived Eve by his craftiness, so your minds may be corrupted from the simplicity that is in Christ"** (2 Corinthians 11:3). NKJV.*

# CHAPTER 9:

## EMOTIONS (MOODS AND ATTITUDES)

Emotions are our strong feelings of our state of spirit and mind in times of peace or war or strong feelings in general towards certain things within us or in the environment around us. Overall, we have good or bad feelings all the time over issues affecting us or people around us. As Christians, our feelings are important in our journey with our Lord Jesus Christ. Indeed, emotion is the composition of our attitudes, moods and feelings which can be both positive and negative. Our feelings, attitudes and moods involve things such as joy, love, peace, fear, anger, jealousy, violence, anger, pain, pleasure, interest and so on. Emotions may also include but not be limited to the following: a sense of honour and delight, compassion for others, comfort and satisfaction, intellectual curiosity, and a sense of accomplishment in one's life. Feelings can move us in positive and negative ways which give us a sense of life. Certainly, without feelings, we cannot do what we are doing in life. So yes, indeed feelings are an important part of our lives and we must take good care of them.

Nevertheless, the great power of our feelings in life towards things not only drives us, touches us and moves us, but also encroaches into all areas of our lives and becomes what we do every day. Feelings change everything about our lives and everything about its outcomes. At this stage, one could have abandonment to feelings that carry them away every time over an issue or issues. People who have succumbed to their feelings about things are easily carried away every time certain things happen in their lives or around their close relatives. This is called a state of the deadness of the soul as a person is just moved by emotions. The dead soul is the one that is about to explode or to fall apart, due to the trouble going on around them that they cannot understand. Such a person has no hope in life. Life becomes so desolate that they must be dependent upon satisfaction or addictions.

Simply, feelings of desolate people revolve around being comforted by certain satisfactions that become addictive in life. Things such as adultery, smoking, drinking, violence, gossip, slanders, and drug abuse are because of addictive feelings. The value of life in the addict is placed on feelings that must be satisfied through certain things in life. The feelings in these people's lives are sustained by images and ideas of things that they are dependent upon for satisfaction. For example, when people have suffered abuse and rejection in their lives, inculcated in their minds are the scenes of unkindness, brutality, worthlessness, and lack of longing sometimes for life. Their whole world is structured in their minds in the forms of negative ideas and self-defeating thoughts about themselves.

When one's life becomes structured around strong feelings towards certain things, it forms images and ideas in the minds that are fostered and sustained moods. The moods are feelings that penetrate us and everything around us. Moods for instance are things like anger, fear, pain, and stress which dominate and control our lives. When a person is overtaken by moods, the response to any situation always is through moods. It is fair to say that in the life of these people, God is not in it. When people have lost hope in life and are in a negative trajectory about themselves and their lives, then they know that they have no God in them, because God is of hope, love, and peace.

Nevertheless, our character must also be moulded by the way we feel about ourselves. We must cultivate love, joy and peace within us that shape our character. It is only when we have plenty of peace, love and joy within us that we can share those things with others. In other words, our character is the true image of who we become when others form their decision about us. The biggest challenge to us today is the fact that we try to share the peace, love and joy we have with others, but it is not enough for us. And the effect of this is we always have problems when others do not love us back the way we show them, love. The only way we can love others and get others to love adequately is when we are connected to the fountain of love, peace, and joy, which is Jesus Christ. It is when the spirit of God is poured into us abundantly, we are able to share peace, love, and joy with others.

## God Wants to Control Your Emotions

So, let us now look at the positive parts of our feelings in God. When we have God in our lives our feelings and moods are dominated by hope, love, joy, peace, worthiness, and confidence over things within us and around us. The indispensable love of God over us Christians is the foundation of positive feelings and moods. Undoubtedly there is nothing impossible with God. All the impossibilities of mankind are possibilities of God. Christians' lives are transformed inwardly to be like that of Jesus Christ. The Christian's feelings and moods are dominated by the fruits of the holy spirit; love, joy, peace, goodness, patience, gentleness, self-control, and kindness, and are grounded on faith in God. Hence, no room for negative feelings unless you are not a born-again Christian. Even in the event of trouble, pain and suffering, Christians are never crushed because they are already on a positive trajectory. The Christian faith and hope are important instruments of the Christians' lives. *"Therefore, having been justified by faith, we have peace with God through our Lord Jesus Christ, through whom also we have access by faith into this grace in which we stand, and rejoice in hope of the glory of God. And not only that but we also glory in tribulations, knowing that tribulation produces perseverance; and perseverance, character; and character, hope. Now hope does not disappoint, because the love of God has been poured out in our hearts by the Holy Spirit who was given to us.* (Roman 5:1-5). NKJV.

## Hope and Faith in God

Hope is a strong base for a Christian's faith. Hope is the anticipation of things that have not yet been seen or received from the sovereign being beyond our thoughts, imagination, and our reach – God. Hope is removing the problems we are going through in life and giving them to a sovereign being that has all the capabilities to solve them for us. We as Christians are saved and rejoice in the hope no matter the situations we are facing in life. The hope of the things we have not seen and anticipate from God strengthen us and enable us to be grounded by faith in God. Because we know that God almighty is faithful, and he will never fail those who believe and place their trust in him. For as it is written: *"Eye has not seen, nor ear heard, nor have entered into the heart of man the things which God has prepared for those who love Him."* (1 Corinthians 2:9). NKJV. To think and act like this is our hope as Christians.

Faith is another strong weapon of Christians. Faith is evidence of those things we hope for in God. We know God exists and he will answer our needs. St Paul said, we must not as Christians focus our attention on those things that are seen but rather on those things that are unseen, for the seen came from the unseen. This is our faith as Christians: think like and act like. For example, Abraham was promised the land of Canaan by God, and he died in faith having not received it but it was later on received by his offspring. Sometimes we as Christians are impatient when we are waiting for God, that is why I showed you this example of Abraham, but it may not be the case for some of us who are waiting for a response from God. *"Now faith is the substance of things hoped for, the evidence of things not seen. By it, the elders obtained a good testimony. By faith, we understand that the worlds were framed by the word of God so that the things which are seen were not made of things which are visible"*. **Faith at the Dawn of History.** *"By faith, Abel offered to God a more excellent sacrifice than Cain, through which he obtained witness that he was righteous, God testifying of his gifts; and through it he, being dead still speaks. By faith, Enoch was taken away so that he did not see death, "and was not found, because God had taken him"; for before he was taken, he had this testimony, that he pleased God. But without faith, it is impossible to please Him, for he who comes to God must believe that He is and that He is a rewarder of those who diligently seek Him. By faith Noah, being divinely warned of things not yet seen moved with godly fear prepared an ark for the saving of his household, by which he condemned the world and became heir of the righteousness which is according to faith"*. (Hebrews 11:1-7). NKJV.

## Love

Love is an unconditional feeling and attraction towards a person or people. It is a complete wishing and willing of good over that person or people. Love is planning something good toward the person or people for their welfare. Well, God's love is much bigger than this, as Christ died for us while we were all sinners. This unmatched love of God for human beings is that he died for you and me so that we can have life and have it abundantly. In essence, God's love for mankind has been expressed in all things he created and the dominance he gave mankind over all the creation. The true love of God is shown in his son dying on the cross for us. There is no other love than this in God's process of redemption: he first loved us. If you are a Christian, then know that God loves you and you must abide in his love, when you move closer to him.

When we know that God loves us unconditionally, we must love others. The second great commandment is the love of neighbours as oneself. We must love others unconditionally just as God has loved us unconditionally. True love through Christ has united all Christians around the world despite race, colour, gender, age, power, wealth and geographical locations. As true lovers of Christ, we must not plan and wish bad things against our neighbours. *"Love suffers long and is kind; love does not envy; love does not parade itself, is not puffed up; does not behave rudely, does not seek its own, is not provoked, thinks no evil; does not rejoice in iniquity, but rejoices in the truth; bears all things, believes all things, hopes all things, endures all things. Love never fails. But whether there are prophecies, they will fail; whether there are tongues, they will cease; whether there is knowledge, it will vanish away"* (1Corinthians 13:4-8). NKJV.

# Joy

Joy is a sense of complete well-being in oneself. It is a lot deeper and broader than any pleasure. Because joy is a state of well-being even in the middle of suffering, pain and loss. Joy is when everything around us looks bad there is still the innermost feeling transformation into the Christlikeness within us. St Paul argued that Christians must always rejoice in the Lord no matter what circumstances we are in.

# Peace

Peace is the state of not being annoyed through worry, problems, thoughts, and unwanted actions within us or around us on how things may turn out. The peace between us and God was restored through the crucifixion of Jesus Christ on the cross for us. By his death on the cross, we are assured of outcomes of things in life as we are redeemed, justified, sanctified, and reconciled to God. In this, we are made righteous to qualify for his grace, glory and mercy that enable us to get what we want from him.

## Satan Also Wants to Control Your Emotions

# Fear

There are two fears all Christians go through in life. They are fear of God and fear of Satan. The fear of God is encouraged whereas the fear of Satan must be overcome. Fear of God is to not be afraid of things in life but rather to be afraid of his laws, statutes and commandments to avoid his wrath and anger for you. It is a healthy fear that knowing his character and attributes will bring his blessings to you and other benefits. For example, fear of God gives you his wisdom and understanding, which leads to life, rest, peace and love in him for your salvation. It is also a source of the fountain of our security in him.

In contrast, the fear of Satan is the dangerous one that terrorises us and is intended for evil overcoming our lives. Satan uses fear as the number one weapon to immobilise us. The "spirit of fear" completely takes over our lives in the forms of sickness, divorce, loss of job, financial crisis, childlessness, depression, mistrust, cheating, adultery, natural disasters, wars, starvation, death and future vision and mission. Listen to me: these are all unnecessary fears Satan brings into your life to crush your spirit. By doing so you will lose confidence and hope in yourself. By doing this he wants you to believe that your life is out of control, and you can never put it back together. This fear is abbreviated as; false evidence appearing real (F.E.A.R).

Besides, fear may also come from within us; the things we have done wrong in the past. This fear within us, clings to us from our own sins we have committed, and the sense of guilt created thereafter, which Satan can use strongly against us. These guilty feelings may be about people we have wronged, cheated, abused, or unmet expectations, failed exams, depression, stress, anxiety and many disappointments in one's life. If this, is you then you must confess, repent and seek God for forgiveness. You do not have to live that way. There is no sin God cannot forgive, so do not let the devil deceived you into acceptance of that guilt.

Finally, the only way we can overcome Satan's fear is by placing our confidence, love and trust in God. This is what you must know; love has no fear. For perfect love drives away fear, for fear is to do with punishment by God. The bible puts it very clear that the one who fears is not made perfect in love. We are not perfect, and our God knows this, and he is the only one who can make us perfect. From the beginning in the book of Genesis all the way to the book of Revelation, God reminds us to "Fear not." For when we submit to him, he is the only force who can thwart the power of Satan. For instance, the book of Isaiah 41:10 encourages Christians, *"Do not fear, for I am with you; Do not anxiously look about you, for I am your God I will strengthen you, surely I will help you, Surely I will uphold you with My righteous right hand."* We always fear the future and what it will bring to us. Hence, Jesus Christ tells us that God even cares for the birds of the air, so how much more will He care and provide for His children (the Christians)? He continues to say, *"Don't be afraid; you are more valuable than a lot of sparrows"* (Matthew 10:31). God teaches us not to be afraid of being alone because he is with us, of being too weak. After all, he is our strength, of not being heard because he hears us, and of lacking physical necessities because he will provide for us. So, fear not, think like it and act like it. So, if you are a Christian and have come across this book, do not let Satan keep you away from God through fear. As King David puts it, it is a valley of the shadow of death. It is not a real thing once you discover your power, your authority, and your identity in Christ.

## Depression

Certainly, depression is one of the most dangerous weapons Satan uses against the believers after fear. Depression gets us into the state of hopelessness (emotions) through self-condemnation, doubt, bad thoughts, and imaginations that plunge us deep into a deadly self-defeating outlook of our future, perhaps leading to suicidal thoughts if not suicide itself. When one thinks or prefers death over life then know that Satan has won against you. Depression is not a new thing in life. Both churches and government leaders go through it. But the good news is that it can be overcome, and you can overcome it as well. In the bible there are no better examples than the ones of King David and St. Paul when they were in the states of depression; ***"In the day of my trouble I sought the Lord; my hand was stretched out in the night without ceasing; my soul refused to be comforted. I remembered God, and was troubled; I complained, and my spirit was overwhelmed. You hold my eyelids open; I am so troubled that I cannot speak".*** (Psalm 77:2–4). ***"We were burdened beyond measure, above strength, so that we despaired even of life"*** **(2 Corinthians 1:8b).**

Depression is a situation or a condition everyone goes through and you must not be the exception, but you must know how to get rid of it. It is fair to say that depression is a situation we cannot avoid in life as we deal with the shocking news of such things as; the death of our loved ones, financial losses, wars, starvation, political upheaval, and natural disasters. The great man of God, Charles Spurgeon said, "I am the subject of depressions of spirit so fearful that I hope none of you ever get to such extremes of wretchedness as I go to. "The only way you can win against depression is to put your trust in God. Whatever you are worried about, put it in the hands of God almighty, for all the impossibilities of humans are his possibilities. He is the one who can solve all your problems. This how you can fight it; ***"Be anxious for nothing, but in everything by prayer and supplication, with thanksgiving, let your requests be made known to God; and the peace of God, which surpasses all understanding, will guard your hearts and minds through Christ Jesus"*** (Philippians 4:6-7). NKJV.

# Doubt

Likewise, when Satan gets you depressed, he gets you to doubt all sources for your help in order to kill you. Whether for example, your self-confidence in getting out of the situation you are in, or the words of counselling by your friends or professional counsellors or God helping you through a reading of the bible, Satan gets you to doubt them all. He paints this picture in your mind that; you are defeated, you will never recover from this sickness, your marriage will never be good again, and more importantly, God does not exist let alone ready to help you. Satan will suggest these thoughts to you: he tried it with Eve in the Garden, *"Has God really said?"* (Genesis 3:1); and He tried it with Jesus in the wilderness, *"If You are the Son of God"* (Luke 4:3). Let me assure you as a Christian he will do it for you. Know that you are at war with Satan, whether you like it or not, and you must face up to him in a battle for your life. There is no way you can do this other than the word of God. The Bible is our radar and compass to guide us during our difficult and trying moments. Never give in to doubt, recognise it as a weapon of the devil and get rid of it. For when you doubt you will never get anything or help from God. St James put it very clearly; **"But let him ask in faith, with no doubting, for he who doubts is like a wave of the sea driven and tossed by the wind. For let, not that man suppose that he will receive anything from the Lord; he is a double-minded man, unstable in all his ways"** (James 1:6-8). NKJV.

# Unforgiveness

Unforgiveness is refusing to let go in your heart and mind all the toxic abuses, hates, grudges, shames, bad decisions and mistakes you have committed against yourself and other people. God wants you to forgive yourself and other people so that when you come to him in prayer, you have an untroubled conscience - guilty of sins. You must forgive all the people; the ones you have offended and the ones who have offended you. I know it is one of the hardest things to do and particularly to those who have offended you without your provocation. To be honest with you I have struggled with it for a very long time special in forgiving those who have offended me without my provocation. So, it is not you alone, but you must forgive if you want to be healthy and require God blessings.

Before I stated why God wants you to forgive, let me say why it is good to forgive for your good health in our natural understanding. Firstly, holding all the toxics hates against someone in your heart, breaks down your spirit. Which in turn, broke down your flesh and bones. So Unforgiveness can be caused by some of the diseases we have today in our bodies like arthritis and much more. This is not a made-up story; it is scientifically proven. Secondly, it limits opportunities in sharing knowledge, abilities and skills you would have had with that person had you been in a peaceful relationship including future opportunities you might need help from that person. So, in the natural world, we must learn to admit our mistakes and wrongs, we have done to each other - apologise and move on together for a better future together.

Here is why God wants you to forgive; firstly so that you are also forgiven by him. Remember we are all sinners, and if you do not forgive others, God will never forgive you your sins. Jesus Christ died for us all while we were all sinners including the ones you hate. Secondly, he wants no sin to be used against you by Satan in the court of heaven to hinder his blessing for you. These claims can also be backed up in the Lord pray; forgive us our sins as we forgive those who have sinned against us. Listen to me very carefully; God cannot bless a sinful heart. God does not need a single person in hell, and so why waste time holding grudges and hates against people. You must forgive so that you are placed in a better position for God's miracle.

# CHAPTER 10:

## OUR SOUL IF SAVED WILL GO TO HEAVEN AND IF NOT SAVED, TO HELL WHEN WE DIE

Our soul is a composition of our wills, minds, and emotions. Our soul is the important determiner of what we can do in our lives. It dictates what our bodies and spirits do. So, you can see how important your soul is to the spiritual forces of good or evil. That is why both sides are after it day and night to control it. The spirit who controls your soul controls you. We also know that in the ideal natural world, who the man thinks he is, he becomes. What you are so determined to do is what you can do. The disheartening thing is that many people do not know that they are at war with forces of good and evil for their soul. Well, if you have not noticed before, then note now that you are at war with Satan, your adversary for your soul. We are in spiritual warfare. The battle to take your mind, and to thereafter control you is fought over you by the Godhead – God, Jesus Christ, the Holy Spirit and all the angels of heaven against the forces of Satan, his angels, and demons. It is a war between God almighty your creator who has a good plan for you and Satan your adversary who has a bad plan for you.

The spiritual warfare battle to control our minds starts with thoughts. What the world has not explained clearly or questioned is where these thoughts come from. The human mind is invaded by thoughts on a daily basis, which gets into our spirits and becomes the dominant power that operates in us for good or bad. The thoughts that come from God are received into our spirits by God's spirit (the holy spirit) and he relays them to our soul for the decision-making process that may reject or receive them. Once the soul makes the decisions for the thoughts to stay, the soul sends them back into our spirits, and they become our thoughts. The thoughts that come from Satan are received into our bodies through the five senses and relay to our souls for decision making whether to be received or rejected by our souls. For example, Satan will bring fear to us through thoughts in our minds from what we have seen happening around us, sickness with the pains in our bodies or the reports we receive from the doctors about the state of our bodies, accidents, war, bad weather, and news of the death of our loved ones. The strongest weapon used by Satan against us is fear. When fear gets hold of us it gets into our spirits and breaks us down. When either good or bad thoughts get into us they become strongholds in our lives that can take us to heaven or hell. Hence, the choices we make in this life determine whether we can go to heaven or hell. Within your mind, you can know whether you are destined for heaven or hell by the choices you make in this life and the lifestyle you live. So, going to heaven or hell is predictable now before you die.

## God Wants to Control You by Controlling Your Soul

Pay attention to this; God will never trust you until you have surrendered your soul to him. You may ask me, why is this? Because he was betrayed by mankind in the garden of Eden when Adam sided with Satan over God. Furthermore, God will never use you until you are obedient and willing to work for him. Your faith in God remains a claim until you are tested to prove to God, that you are worthy of heaven. Many Christians do not know that they are at war with Satan until they cross over from the Satanic kingdom to God's Kingdom. Satan being the tempter will throw at you all his wiles and darts to give up on God. He will use every single weapon available to him whether it is fear, doubt, unforgiveness, unbelief, sickness, wars, and natural disasters to break you down or even to kill you. No single person who is a Christian is immune from this when they choose to follow Christ. The reason why God allows Satan to tempt you is to crucify your works of the flesh that you might live to righteousness. I came under Satanic attacks in the form of sickness, childlessness, unemployment, and natural disasters from my young age until now, but I must not give up on God. The good news is that God will never allow Satan to tempt you beyond what you are able to bear. So, the earth is the war zone where we live. But the good news is that we are the winners of this war as Jesus Christ has already won the battle on our behalf and we must not live as prisoners of war in our souls, spirits, and bodies. God promised to be with us during our tough times and so we must fight the good fight of faith.

When we surrender ourselves to God, the holy spirit of God comes and lives inside of us. The bible teaches us that Jesus Christ came into this world to destroy the work of Satan. So, he has destroyed the works of the Devil in your lives. What you see today in your lives is the shadow of true things. Whatever it is – sickness, poverty, depression, stress, anxiety, addiction and all forms of Satanic attacks will be history if you surrender your life to God. Is not our God wonderful? He can uproot them all and bury them in the deep sea never to be remembered again.

Turn to God so you can live. He is the one who can paralyse the works of Satan in you. This is a warning to us about who is inside of us. We must be conscious of who lives there. If we allow God to live inside of us, we will be carrying his presence everywhere we go to whether it is work, studies, business, or the lifestyle we live. God will make his presence available to us and through us. Your soul is the important determiner of your battles with the Devil, and it must be controlled and operated by God. Your soul determines what you do or doesn't do. God wants our mind to be aligned with the mind of our Lord Jesus Christ in everything we do. Jesus Christ while he was here on earth, was obedient and willing to the point of death in executing the will of his Father God almighty. This is the mind we must have as Christians, who are the followers of Christ. Our minds must be strongholds of righteousness. It can be done!!! It is only in our minds that we can keep God's oracles and stand on his word of love, forgiveness and healing power that shuts up or keep Satan on the periphery of our thoughts, imaginations and emotions.

The strongest weapon to keep Satan at bay from your minds in order not to influence your thoughts is the word of God (the bible). The saddest thing today with many Christians is that they do not have a bible in their homes let alone read it and apply it to their daily issues inflicted on them by Satan. Here is the secret. The bible is the word of God, which was written by prophets and disciples, who were inspired by the holy spirit. When you speak its words over your condition it is no longer you who speaks but God. Can you believe this? Let me take you a little bit further on another mystery. The word of God is Jesus Christ. So when you speak it, you are not speaking the word but it is a person who promised to set you free from all the conditions you might find yourself in. Remember he came to set you free from all the oppression of Satan. Once Satan discovers that you know this secret, he will have no choice, but to comply with what you speak. Also, when you pray you must also speak your words in line with the word of God in the bible. It is by doing so that your will is aligned with the will of God for your life. And I can assure you that nothing will stop you from victory to victory over the temptations of Satan in your life.

## Satan Wants to Control You by Controlling Your Soul

Before we discuss this, let me ask you this question; Why does Satan want to control your soul? The answer is simple; so that you can work for him. But it is a dangerous thing to work with Satan and for Satan as he is your adversary. What got him into trouble in heaven in the first place was the creation of you (mankind). He is up to no good at all as he will steal, kill and destroy your soul in hell. The ongoing physical wars today in the world are not natural wars but spiritual wars caused by the forces of darkness through men and women whose thoughts and imaginations have been controlled and occupied by Satan, his angels and demons. The worst strategy used by Satan has been the control of men and women who occupy high positions of power and authority today in human societies, businesses, and governments, who make unrighteous decisions that cause nations to slide to wars and who have also contributed to the collapse of moral standards of human society. This has also led to the rise of social evils such as same-sex marriage, abortion, and pornography.

When Satan wants to control the other important parts of you such as will and body, he must first control your soul (will, thoughts, imagination, and emotions). So, all that you do is no longer you making a decision but Satan who controls you. Some people may find it very difficult to believe this but let me tell you as you have a body that requires some needs, an eye that you look for attraction and displeasures and ambitions to succeed as tools used by Satan to entice you to sin. You will never miss Satan, as all of these are some of his baits that get you in and possibly lock you in permanently to hell.

*"For the flesh lusts against the Spirit, and the Spirit against the flesh; and these are contrary to one another so that you do not do the things that you wish. Now the works of the flesh are evident, which are: adultery, fornication, uncleanness, lewdness, idolatry, sorcery, hatred, contentions, jealousies, outbursts of wrath, selfish ambitions, dissensions, heresies, envy, murders, drunkenness, revelries, and the like; of which I tell you beforehand, just as I also told you in time past, that those who practice such things will not inherit the kingdom of God"* **Galatians 5:17,19-21 NKJV.**

When one is about to commit the crime, it starts with one or two of the above thoughts. In the case of King David for example, one evening he arose from his bed and walked on the roof of his house when he saw a beautiful woman bathing in an adjacent house. He was tempted to have an affair with her. Just from the moment of his eyes encountering the woman, a lust arose inside him in the form of the thought to go to bed with her. So, what he saw with his eyes became a source of his downfall in the presence of God by committing adultery, betrayal and murder, and that cost him dearly in his family. Through this sin he committed he opened the door for the devil to destroy his family; one of his sons slept openly with his wife and his other son slept with his daughter. Hence, David's adultery became a disaster for the whole family.

When things get off track in our lives it starts with a thought. Before you get addicted to anything in life it starts with a thought. Everything you do or every encounter you make with people starts with a thought. When thoughts get into our soul, they become the source of our success or problems. When thoughts become the source of our success, we are happy but when they become the source of our problems, we are sad. When the thoughts in our minds come from the devil, they cause us problems that most people think can be fixed through alcohol, drugs, cigarettes, and pornography, which they assume will bring them the peace of mind they once had. When most people are in this state of mind they easily blame, circumstances, and people, but the real culprit behind this is Satan. All these thoughts become strongholds of Satan which you cannot get rid of without the help of God and his word. Below are the verses in the bible telling us this; "***For the weapons of our warfare are not carnal but mighty in God for pulling down strongholds, casting down arguments and every high thing that exalts itself against the knowledge of God, bringing every thought into captivity to the obedience of Christ, and being ready to punish all disobedience when your obedience is fulfilled***". 2 Corinthians 10:4-6. (NKJV).

That is how badly both God and Satan want to control your soul to control you. Once unclean spirits control you, Satan controls what you can do for him that determines your destiny for hell. Obviously, God wants to control our souls for good. When this happens, we are destined for heaven. Having said this I will discuss or bring to your attention one stronghold of the devil that if you are not careful may still take us to hell, and that is the unforgiveness of sins. You may ask why I am concerned about this? Well, if you do not forgive others then God will never forgive you. Simple as that. And when God does not forgive us then we miss our salvation. Very important indeed. Listen to this carefully, "If God is the lord of all creations, then he must be the lord of all the things you need including the salvation of our souls. If there is one thing that will make you a friend of God, then it is the forgiveness of sins, because while we were all sinners Christ died for us all.

## What is the Forgiveness of Sins?

It is the ability to let go of all those mistakes you have committed against yourself and others. It is a complete obliteration in your systems – mind, and heart–all the toxic hate, bitterness, and anger against yourself and others. Forgive and never remember. That is the true meaning of forgiveness, and this is what qualifies us for heaven.

All of us want God's blessings, but not all of us know the ways in which we can get God's blessings. We all want a happy family, good health, a better job, a successful career, love, peace, joy, salvation, and eternal life, yet it all remains wishful thinking to us because we do not know how to get them. Sometimes we may be favoured by God to get some of these things we want so easily and so we do not appreciate them and what God has done for us.

Forgiveness is a two- way thing; you must first forgive yourself for those wrong decisions you have made that have failed you, the wrong career you chose that has never given you the job of your heart, the wrong relationship you went into that does not work, the wrong friendship that you established in which you have been backstabbed, the gossip, offence, and slander you did with your friends for which you were caught by the victim, the murder you have committed, the attempted suicide on your life because life has lost meaning to you, the adultery you have committed with someone's wife/husband and so forth.

Secondly, you must forgive others who have wronged you; the gossip, slander and offensive words people have labelled against you to destroy your reputation, the wrongs investment decisions you have made that have affected your financial position through the financial brokers, the divorce you have just gone through and you are not sure how your life will go after it, the family members who have disowned you, those drugs you consumed that have given you nightmares, that alcohol you take which has robbed your family of their finances and so forth.

We sometimes take the forgiveness of sins lightly and this may be because we do not know the consequences of sins when we are so determined not to forgive. Before Christ came to die for us, every single sin committed by every single person required an animal sacrifice or punishment by death. In other words, someone had to die for his sin, or else an animal had to die on his behalf for his sins to be forgiven by God. That is how serious God was for the punishment of sins.

When Christ came, things had to change, he had to die for our sins all for God to forgive us and to reconcile us back to himself. But even as he has died for us, one thing has not changed; the forgiveness of sins that remains conditional for going to heaven. God has forgiven you for your sins and so you must also forgive others who have wronged you to have your salvation. And that is a condition of exchange for your forgiveness of others to receive your salvation.

You might think God has turned a blind eye on the sins you just committed but guess what? The devil has not. Immediately once you commit a sin, he goes to God to seek permission for torment. For the sins we continue to commit against ourselves and God, we must repent quickly or else the devil will come to discipline us if we do not repent, and take us to hell with him. For example, people today continue to face unnecessary fear, guilt, alienation, shame, stress, disappointment, suicide, mental problems, eternal condemnation, and so forth because they are not willing to forgive and repent of their sins. Unfortunately, the devil will torment them until they die.

Once you are dead without God, that is it – you will end in hell forever. Have you ever asked yourself where this destruction is coming from? Well, it is from the sin you have just committed, that you have not repented of. This must be a red flag for you. Going to heaven is not free in the way we think.

*"The wages of sin is death, but the gift of God is eternal life through Jesus Christ"* **Romans 6:23.**

*"The wicked will go to eternal fire prepared for the devil and his angels"* **Matthew 25:41.**

*"To be heirs of the hope of eternal life, we must be justified by God's grace"* Titus 3:7.

# PART III: SPIRIT

## The Channel of Communication With God

What God created in His own image and his own likeness is the human spirit. What makes humankind unique from other living and nonliving things is his spirit. This begs the question; Why did God create mankind in his own image and his own likeness? The answer to this question is for communication purposes. We know God is a spirit, and so far, we have seen that both body and soul are not spirit and have no abilities and capabilities to communicate with God. Therefore, besides body and soul, God had to add the spirit to us for us to communicate with him. But not only that, God, has also given us (human beings), dominion over all his creation on earth and there is a need for us to communicate with him. For example, God had to bring created animals to Adam for naming including Adam's wife Eve, who was given a name by Adam. Let us prove this claim in the bible.

Genesis 1:26-27 – *"Then God said, "Let Us make man in Our image, according to Our likeness; let them have dominion over the fish of the sea, over the birds of the air, and over the cattle, over all the earth and over every creeping thing that creeps on the earth." So,*

## THE MANIFESTATION OF A PERSON WHO CONTINUES TO LIVE BY FLESH AND NOT BY THE SPIRIT

### LIVING ACCORDING TO THE FLESH
1 Corinthians 3:3 carnal 'Christians' behaving like mere men; 3:16 "Do you not know that you are the temple of God and that the Spirit of God dwells in you?"

**FLESH** (Rom. 8:8)
The ingrained habit patterns still appeal to the mind to live independent of God.

**BODY**
Tension or migraine headaches, nervous stomach, hives, skin rashes, allergies, asthma, some arthritis, spastic colon, heart palpitations, respiratory ailments, etc.

*a human mind and the mind of the spirit*

**MIND**
Double-minded

**SPIRIT** (Rom. 8:9)
Alive but quenched (1 Thess. 5:19)

*the born again person has a spirit born of the Holy Spirit*

**EMOTIONS**
Unstable

*driven by the natural man - the old unregenerated man*

*but the sons of God are led by the Holy Spirit*

walk after the flesh (often)

immorality
impurity
sensuality
idolatry
sorcery
enmities
strife
jealousy
outbursts of anger
disputes
dissensions
factions
envying
drunkenness
carousing

*Fruits of the flesh; flesh and blood cannot enter the kingdom of God*

walk after the Spirit (seldom)

love
joy
peace
patience
kindness
goodness
faithfulness
gentleness
self-control

*Fruits of the Spirit*

*https://citizenheaven.wordpress.com*

***God created man in His own image; in the image of God He created him; male and female He created them."*** So, this verse is proof that God created mankind in his own image and his own likeness. This verse is not only important for us to understand ourselves and our origin but also what happened that day when Adam and Eve ate from the tree of knowledge of good and evil. We know that God is not a body and soul but a spirit. So, our spirit was created out of God's spirit. John 4:24- ***"God is Spirit, and those who worship Him must worship in spirit and truth."*** You cannot worship God in your body and soul but in your spirit as it is made of his image and his likeness (his Spirit). For instance, you cannot receive the information or messages from the radio or television stations or outlets unless you have radio and television in your house or around you. In the same way, you cannot receive information from God unless your spirit is connected to the spirit of God. Your body and soul are limited only to your five senses operation; when it comes to the things of God you need your spirit to be connected through the help of the Holy Spirit. The Spirit of God is your connector to the things of God, and you must allow him to live in you permanently. On many occasions, many people want to connect to God using their souls. You cannot understand things of spirit using your own wisdom. It does not work.

This is clearly explained by St. Paul in the book of 1 Corinthians 2:14 – ***"But the natural man does not receive the things of the Spirit of God, for they are foolish to him; nor can he know them, because they are spiritually discerned."*** St. Paul is saying here that one cannot understand things of spirit using body and soul without the spirit's involvement. No matter what, you cannot understand things of God using your five senses (sight, smell, taste, hearing and touch), and your Soul (imagination, creativity, wisdom and emotions). It does not work unless your spirit is involved. In this verse, the word "natural" is the Greek adjective "psuchikos" from the word "psuchi" which means soul. So, a person who has a soul or uses their soul to understand things of God is called a natural man or woman. To this effect when you use your body and soul you cannot receive from God.

Furthermore, it is the same spirit given to us that will go back to God when we die. God is immortal (deathless), by nature. God has also given us Christians the same immortality as those who believe in him. Luke 20:34-38 – *"Jesus answered and said to them, 'The sons of this age marry and are given in marriage. But those who are counted worthy to attain that age, and the resurrection from the dead, neither marry nor are given in marriage, nor can they die anymore, for they are equal to the angels and are sons of God, being sons of the resurrection".* But even Moses showed in the burning bush passage that the dead are raised when he called the Lord 'the God of Abraham, the God of Isaac, and the God of Jacob.' *"For He is not the God of the dead but of the living, for all live to Him."*

Our human spirits were created by God purposely for communication with him. Our spirits are where the spirit of God (the holy spirit), communes with us. It is our spirits that can be born again with the spirit of God. It is our spirits that relate with the spirit of God, giving us deep revelations of God-knowledge. It is within our spirits that the holy spirit moves to teach us things of God and convict us of sins.

Right away from the book of Genesis, we can see that God created us with this human spirit. Genesis 2:7 says, *"Jehovah God formed man from the dust of the ground and breathed into his nostrils the breath of life, and man became a living soul."*

The human spirit in this verse can be seen here as we break down your body into body, soul and spirit- "the dust of the ground" becomes the physical body, "a living soul" is your soul, which is your psychological part of you, your mind, your emotion, and your will. "The breath of life"- is your human spirit. This is clearly stated and backed up by the book of Proverbs 20:27, *"The spirit of man is the lamp of Jehovah."*

# CHAPTER 11:

## SPIRIT CREATED IN THE IMAGE OF GOD

⟵——⟩)•((——⟶

### Spiritual Man (Spirit-Filled Man)

Spirit man is an immortal person (he does not die). This is true that you were created out of God's image. Your spirit came from God. He will go back to God if you are saved and to hell if you are condemned. For your spirit to go back to God your spirit must be born again of the holy spirit of God. This means your spirit must be connected to the holy spirit of God to communicate, receive and understand things of God. **NKJV** John 3:5-8 – *"Jesus answered, 'Most assuredly, I say to you unless one is born of water and the Spirit, he cannot enter the kingdom of God. That which is born of the flesh is flesh, and that which is born of the Spirit is spirit. Do not marvel that I said to you, 'You must be born again.' The wind blows where it wishes, and you hear the sound of it, but cannot tell where it comes from and where it goes. So is everyone who is born of the Spirit.'"* Meaning: Jesus Christ is the way, the truth, and the life. Unless you accept Jesus Christ as the son of God and your personal saviour, there is no other way to God. This is a truth you must accept if you love your life. **NKJV John 14:6 –** *"Jesus said to him, 'I am the way, the truth, and the life. No one comes to the Father except through Me'".*

The spiritual person's body is where the spirit of God sits and operates to communicate with heaven (the Godhead). When your spiritual senses are born with the holy spirit of God, all your spiritual body senses begin to operate perfectly to comprehend what heaven is trying to communicate to you here on earth daily. It is your spiritual body that gives you the ability to eat, talk, walk, smell, taste, and all other functions you perform as a human being here on earth, and when it leaves your natural body, your natural body remains as dust to be put back into the ground/earth. And for your spiritual body to go back to heaven, it must now be connected to heaven while you are still alive or else Satan will take it to hell to await judgement from there when you die. It is the holy spirit who raised Jesus Christ from the dead, who must also raise you from death and you must be born of him.

The spirit-filled person upon being born of the holy spirit of God becomes a true Christian and shall receive the gift of the holy spirit. The holy spirit shall dwell inside the born-again Christian. The evidence that the holy spirit is dwelling inside a person is by the fruits of the spirit of god. The person that has the indwelling of the holy spirit in his life should reflect Christ, as he has the mind of Christ. **Galatians 5:22- says, "But the fruit of the Spirit is love, joy, peace, longsuffering, kindness, goodness, faithfulness, gentleness, self-control. Against such there is no law".** And those *who are* Christ's have crucified the flesh with its passions and desires. If we live in the Spirit, let us also walk in the Spirit. This person now lives righteously, and they are confident that they are saved. **2 Timothy 4 says, "*I have fought the good fight,*

*I have finished the race, I have kept the faith. Finally, there is laid up for me the crown of righteousness, which the Lord, the righteous Judge, will give to me on that Day, and not to me only but also to all who have loved His appearing".* You are not a natural body that returns to dust after death, but a spiritual body that goes back to God if you are saved, or to hell if you are not saved after death. Now is the time to decide where you belong, to God or Satan? There is no middle ground.

## The Spirit-Filled Man Feeds on the Word of God

Do we live to eat or do we eat to live? The answer is: we live to eat. Because the spirit-man was first created before the body-man. Jesus Christ Said, a man should not live on bread alone but from every word that proceeds out from God's mouth. The food of the spirit-filled man is the word of God. Ultimately also the parable of the rich fool teaches us that; "the ground of a certain rich man yielded plentifully. "and he thought within himself, saying, 'what shall I do since I have no room to store my crops?' "So, he said, 'I will do this: I will pull down my barns and build greater, and there I will store all my crops and my goods. 'And I will say to my soul, "Soul, you have many goods laid up for many years; take your ease; eat, drink, and be merry. "But God said to him, 'Fool! Tonight, your soul will be required of you; then whose will those things be which you have provided?' "So is he who lays up treasure for himself and is not rich toward God." Furthermore, according to the scriptures, it is clear that God had predestined you and me. God foreknew you and me before we were conceived in our mother's wombs." God said; Let us make mankind in our own image." God is a spirit and who created you and I first as spirits in heaven before he wrapped us into our mothers' wombs to be conceived as bodies. So, when you and I are born, we are born as spirits in the bodies.

Watch this very carefully; when you and I were born, God had already finished his work. He had already declared both the beginning and the end of you and me in heaven. That is why everything whether good or bad that happened to you and me here on earth do not come as a surprise to God. Those things whether good or bad which happened to you and me along our ways are not there to crush us but rather to shape us into our final destinations." All things worked together for good to those who love God and those who are chosen for his purpose."

Before you and I became bodies, God had already assigned you and me jobs we will come and do on earth. A good example here is Prophet Jeremiah who was given his assignment as a prophet before he even became a body (person). The world called your assignment your passion, whereas God called your assignment your mission here on earth. You must stop looking for your assignment from people and seek God for it. He has it for you. Every single person on this planet is not an accident, you have a purpose of which God created you. And you must find your purpose within you. God has already put it in there. Do not look to others, look to yourself. When you have found your purpose within you, you will have value and people will come to you because of your unique gifts within you. It is important to note that God does not necessarily need every single person to be a preacher of his word, but rather his sons who fear him and to work in other disciplines which may require his work. God wants to raise politicians, doctors, lawyers, scientists, leaders and businessmen who love him and love other fellow human beings.

## The Spirit-Filled Man Fears God

It depends on a person or people's understanding of what is really the fear of God. Others take the fear of God as respect for him, and others take it as a complete terror of him on them. On the contrary, also others think it is unnecessary in this age of grace brought about by the reconciliation of mankind back to God through the blood and flesh of Jesus Christ. I personally think that none of the above views represents the true fear of God. Fear of God is deeper and bigger than the above views. Fearing God means doing his will. Those who fear God listen, obey, and do whatever God says, whether it is clear or not. It is an absolute commitment to his laws, commandments, statutes, and judgments. It is living in the world following the rules and regulations of the kingdom of heaven on earth. For example, no one-likes children being disobedient to their parents. This also is the same with God; he does not like children who are disobedient to him. Unfortunately, there are some Christians today who do not want a one-on-one relationship with God but only go to him at the time of their needs and stop there. This should be the right way of seeking God: that we have a deeper relationship with God, seeking first above all else, the kingdom of God and its righteousness and everything else shall be added to us by him. It is when you have a deeper relationship with God that you will experience his deliverance, prosperity, health, vision and mission, power, glory, honour, wisdom, and strength. Isn't he a good God when he can give you all of these things on earth?

# Natural Man

The "Natural Man" is a person who is born with a sinful nature. Galatians 5 says, *"Now the works of the flesh are evident, which are: adultery, fornication, uncleanness, lewdness, idolatry, sorcery, hatred, contentions, jealousies, outbursts of wrath, selfish ambitions, dissensions, heresies, envy, murders, drunkenness, revelries, and the like; of which I tell you beforehand, just as I also told you in time past, that those who practice such things will not inherit the kingdom of God".*

The natural person has a natural body (formed out of the dust of the ground and depends on natural food to operate). This person does not understand things of God, nor does he believe them, because he is not born of God but of flesh. This person is typically a person born with a self-centred belief in himself. This person has no fear of God, as he is born in sin, live in and will die in sin. However, if this person is willing and wants to be taught right from wrong according to the Bible; he may choose to accept or resist. Furthermore, this person may also be taught by the holy spirit of God on the knowledge of good and evil, but he may choose to accept or resist. But he must not deny one fact that the laws of knowledge of good and evil are within him, written in his heart by God. That is why he must be subject to judgement at the end of things when Jesus Christ will come to judge both the dead and living. So, he has no choice but to rather believe in God before he dies, for one hundred and twenty years of him living on earth, are nothing at all to God-who will judge him in the afterlife. If he cannot find God now in this life, then he will find God in the spirit life thereafter. In short, the things of God are foolishness to this natural man.

This person from the day he is born to the day he will die is called a natural man, a person of the earth, the "old man". He is a person at the centre of his universe believing in theories and literature written by his fellow humans. His work is that of an independent person who has nothing to fear because he does not recognise the creator of the universe (God). His life is centred on his self-desires comforting himself with the company of others, and putting his hope in others, getting ahead, being somebody, prideful in nature, lust, sex, pleasures, and money, rather than God. This person is a God of himself alone and nothing else beyond this life. Sometimes such a person may be willing to help other people by doing charitable work and religious works out of love of humanity, but he does not submit to God, knowing little about what is the will of God for him. This person is the lord of his own righteousness with the use of his conscience. He has his own ideas of right and wrong. But let me say this, if you are one of those doing this, know from me today that it is a dangerous move which will end with catastrophe for your life. You may look like you are a good and honest person, but you are not submitted to God's righteousness. Works and attitudes of the flesh are not of God, and you are not covered by the blood of Jesus Christ that gives you grace for your salvation. What you are doing is dead work and nothing will stop you from going to hell and thereafter the furnace of the unimaginable suffering forever and ever. In this condition, you cannot have true communion and communication with God. You cannot enter heaven and dwell with God in this condition unless you are born again of the spirit of God. You cannot enter heaven without denying self-righteousness to qualify for the grace of God. You cannot enter heaven without a childlike-manner, humility, submissiveness, and trusting and relying on Jesus Christ, the son of the living God.

You will be judged on the knowledge and information brought to you and available to you at that particular time of your death on earth. And as a matter of fact, you need to undergo an inner change, which comes from God's mercy, grace, and glory. The result of this inner change is when a person becomes born again. You must be born of the Holy Spirit of God to communicate, receive, understand, and more importantly gain the salvation of your soul and spirit. Time is up, do not wait for long as Jesus Christ is due to appear any time from now going forward. Never miss your salvation because of your lack of knowledge. Read your bible and the spirit of God will meet you from there. The fact that you refuse to read the bible is an indication that you have already lost the battle of your soul and spirit to Satan.

# CHAPTER 12:

## SPIRIT AS A RECEIVING AERIAL FROM GOD

Arm yourself with his mindset; that while we were all sinners Jesus Christ died for us to set us free from all the sins of our human father – Adam. "Whatever you are going through is a shadow of the true state you should be in. Jesus Christ has done it all. Shun all these demonic lies and turn to God and you will see his wonderful miracle through you and from you. It is never too late. The miracle is in your mouth. How to obtain your miracle:

### Your Human Will

God said, surrender your will to me and have hope in me and you will be set free. The world says: Where there is a Will there is a way. What does this imply about you? It means that God has given you a powerful weapon to use in making your decisions and choosing your choices very carefully, to have a better future. Your human will (which is a part of your soul in other words), is a powerful tool you can use to resist both God and Satan. Your will is your true identity in God, that he gave you to rule the world and to subdue it.

So, the good news to you is that you have your will with you, no matter what situation you are in, you can use it, to get out of that situation. Yes indeed, you can ask me, how is it possible; in this difficult family relationship, in this deadly sickness, I am going through, in this financial situation I am in, in this untreatable condition of childlessness, in this situation of poverty I am in, in this accident which has broken my bones and has damaged my internal organs? Yes, indeed they are the true conditions of the state of your body now, but they are not the conditions God your creator wants you to be in. And if you can just turn to your God you will be set free. He is the Lord who solves all the impossibilities of mankind.

Please use your will to get you out of your situation by telling yourself: This is not the situation my God wants me in, and I must get out of it by putting my hope in him again. Do that and I guarantee you he will never fail in the promise of his good plan for you. Have hope in the living God of heaven and you will see his wonders in changing your situation, in a miraculous way.

## Pure Heart

Jesus Christ said; Blessed are pure in heart, for they shall see God. The world says: great are the men with a pure conscience. You cannot see God until you have met this condition. What does it mean to have a pure heart? It means you must love God with all your heart, mind and your spirit. This practically means that you must completely surrender your will to him, so that it is no longer what you want to do for yourself, but what God wants to do through you, for you and others. Once you have surrendered your will to God, you are now willing, loyal, and obedient to him to follow his instructions, not your instructions. Furthermore, at this point, you can respect and follow his laws, statutes, judgement and commandments. Now the relationship has been established and God can trust you and you can also trust God. Now you have given room for God in your heart to dwell within you, it is no longer a home for demons but God. Whether the demons like it or not, they will automatically go.

The pure heart also means to do good to others. Love your neighbour as yourself. You must show love, peace, kindness and so much more at all times to your neighbours. And who are your neighbours? This could be your wife, husband, children and other people. It also means that you don't have to have a wicked plan in your heart against other people. It practically means that you must not hate, be jealous, and excessively angry against your neighbours. Whether you like it or not these things are all a playing ground for the devil. When you pray to God with these sins in your heart, God will never listen to your prayers as they are a waste of his time. All of us are sinners, with myself included who is giving you this message. When you pray, acknowledge your sins and repent of them before God. Because he knows everything in your heart, and you must not hide from him what he already knows. You must shun all evil in your heart so that you can have your miracle.

## Fear of God

Fear is one of the strongest weapons the devil uses against you to crush you. To instil fear into you, Satan will attack the most important things to you in your life such as your husband, wife, children and other members, finances, health, business, and your other social structures with diseases, accidents, and unexplained tragic death. By doing this he can easily kill your hope, soul, and spirit. Once you have a broken soul and spirit you are done. You begin to be disappointed and discouraged in life in this world. Now daily you become stressed, depressed, and hopeless. You begin to speak to yourself like this; "I will never recover from this sickness, I will never be rich, I will never have a peaceful relationship again, I will never have children, I will never have a job again and I will never get married again" and so much more. From here to you, death is inevitable, but I have come to tell you that this is all lies. There is a way forward from here and in all these lies.

Here is how you can counter all these lies; God has not given you a spirit of fear, but power, love and a sound mind. So, you must not fear no matter what condition the devil put you in. That Jesus Christ has died on the cross on your behalf taking with him all your sins and you are set free by his blood.

Like I said before, God is closer to you at your difficult moments than you think, and all you can do is call out to him as he is already aware of your condition. "Never give the devil a chance to kill you – learn to fight him back. Your miracle is in your mouth.

## Forgiveness of Sins

**"Be kind to one another, tender-hearted, forgiving one another, as God in Christ forgave you" (Ephesians 4:32).**

The main reason we cannot receive from God is due to unforgiveness. There is no substitute for unforgiveness, God has forgiven us our sins and we must be in a position to forgive others their sins. Not only does unforgiveness keep you away from enjoying the blessings of God it also gives Satan ground in your life. The only way we can keep Satan at bay is to forgive other people for their wrongdoings against us by doing good to them. The Bible warns us not to pay evil with evil. When we pay evil with evil, we all become sinners. When we all become sinners, we have no gains from God, and we can perish from our sins. The only way we can overcome evil is to do good to the ones who have wronged us.

Paying the evil with good removes the responsibility of the sin from you and placed it on your offender. When your good action shines on his wrong action, then you have given that person a responsibility for him to look at himself critically. You have given the responsibility to look at his intention, motivation, and wickedness he must correct. Sometimes people provoked us to anger to shame us before the people, but when we do not react negatively in the presence of other people then it is they themselves who are ashamed. Even if people have wronged us, let us continue to greet them nicely from our hearts, provide food for them, visit them when they are sick and pray for them, and more importantly let us continue to chat with them. All these good acts from you will make them feel ashamed and not do bad to you in the future.

Forgiveness is accepting to let go in your heart and mind all the toxic abuses, hates, grudges, shames, bad decisions, and mistakes you have committed against yourself and other people. Sometimes forgiveness does not necessarily mean that we must forgive other people but even ourselves for the bad decisions of the past that continue to haunt us in the present. God wants you to forgive yourself and other people so that when you come to him in prayer, you have an untroubled conscience - guilty of sins. When we have trouble conscience we will never concentrate on our prayers. The devil will continue to remind us of our wrongdoings to others even in the middle of our prayers to distract us. You must forgive all the people; the ones you have offended and the ones who have offended you. I know it is one of the hardest things to do and particularly to those who have offended you without your provocation. To be honest with you I have struggled with it for a very long time, especially in forgiving those who have offended me without my provocation. So, it is not you alone, but you must forgive if you want to be healthy and require God blessings.

Forgiveness is good for you not necessary for others. Before I stated why God wants you to forgive, let me say why it is good to forgive for your good health in our natural understanding. Firstly, holding all the toxics hates against someone in your heart breaks down your spirit. Which in turn broke down your flesh and bones. So Unforgiveness can caused some of the diseases we have today in our bodies like arthritis and much more. This is not a made-up story; it is scientifically proven. Secondly, it limits opportunities in sharing knowledge, abilities, and skills you would have had with that person had you been in a peaceful relationship including future opportunities you might need help from that person. So, in the natural world, we must learn to admit our mistakes and wrongs, we have done to each other - apologise and move on together for a better future together.

God is love and there is no hate in him. If you have found God, then it is easy for you to forgive. Here is why God wants you to forgive; firstly so that you are also forgiven by him. Remember we are all sinners, and if you do not forgive others, God will never forgive you your sins. Jesus Christ died for us all while we were all sinners including the ones you hate. Secondly, he wants no sin to be used against you by Satan in the court of heaven to hinder his blessing for you. These claims can also be backed up in the Lord pray; forgive us our sins as we forgive those who have sinned against us. Listen to me very carefully; God cannot bless a sinful heart. God does not need a single person in hell, and so why waste time holding grudges and hates against people. God considers unforgiveness as a sin and it has the potential to take you to hell if you do not forgive. You must forgive so that you are placed in a better position for God's miracle.

# Faith

Without faith, no one can please God. God wants you to believe in him before you see your miracle. There is a veil between you and God, which is your physical body. Besides, he operates from the supernatural world, and you operate from the natural world. Condition: you must access God in the supernatural world by faith because he is watching you while you are not watching him. **Hebrew 11:1-12 says,** *"Now faith is the substance of things hoped for, the evidence of things not seen. By it, the elders obtained a good testimony. By faith, we understand that the worlds were framed by the word of God so that the things which are seen were not made of visible things. Faith at the Dawn of History By faith Abel offered to God a more excellent sacrifice than Cain, through which he obtained witness that he was righteous, God testifying of his gifts, and through it, he being dead still speaks. By faith, Enoch was taken away so that he did not see death, "and was not found, because God had taken him"; for before he was taken, he had this testimony, that he pleased God. But without faith, it is impossible to please Him, for he who comes to God must believe that He is and that He is a rewarder of those who diligently seek Him. By faith Noah, being divinely warned of things not yet seen, moved with godly fear, prepared an ark for the saving of his household, by which* he condemned the world and became heir of the righteousness which is according to faith. By faith, Abraham obeyed when he was called to go out to the place which he would receive as an inheritance. And he went out, not knowing where he was going. By faith he dwelt in the land of promise as in a foreign country, dwelling in tents with Isaac and Jacob, the heirs with him of the same promise; for he waited for the city which has foundations, whose builder and maker is God. By faith, Sarah herself also received strength to conceive seed, and she bore a child when she was past the age because she judged Him faithful who had promised. Therefore, from one man, and him as good as dead, were born as many as the stars of the sky in multitude—innumerable as the sand which is by the seashore."

## Prayer

God cannot do anything for you unless you pray. God will never intervene in your situation until you pray. If you want God to protect you continually you must pray continually without ceasing. Prayer is the only channel through which you can access all your provisions from God. If you want your sickness to be healed, pray. If you want your family relationship to be restored, pray. Pray- pray- pray to God. I cannot emphasise this enough; God cannot intervene in the affairs of mankind until they pray. Jeremiah 29:11-14 – *"For I know the thoughts that I think toward you, says the Lord, thoughts of peace and not of evil, to give you a future and a hope. Then you will call upon Me and go and pray to Me, and I will listen to you. And you will seek me and find me when you search for Me with all your heart. I will be found by you, says the Lord, and I will bring you back from your captivity; I will gather you from all the nations and from all the places where I have driven you, says the Lord, and I will bring you to the place from which I cause you to be carried away captive."*

## Word of God: the Bible

Please note: It is one thing to hear the word of God, but it also another to do the word of God (this is applying the word to your situation for you to be healed). Furthermore, it is also another thing to hear the voice of God in his word (this means, what does the word say to you concerning your situation for you to have hope and be set free?) Let me tell you this secret: when you recite a bible verse, applying it to the particular area of your need, it is no longer you speaking but God. And if you, do it daily Satan will flee from you because he knows he can no longer hold on to you because it is God who is speaking on your behalf. The word of God can make Satan tremble. You need to read the Bible, meditate on the Word, study the Word, and rightly share the Word. We must take the word of God as medicine to remedy the situation we are in daily until there is a breakthrough (results). If you are sick, please read the following bible passages day and night: Psalm 91, Mark 11:22-24, and Hebrews 9;14-15. If you are in financial difficulty, please read the following bible passages day and night: Proverbs 3:9-10, Malachi 3:10-12, and 2 Corinthians 9;7-12. If you are having family problems, please read the following bible passages day and night: Colossians 3:18-21, Isaiah 54:13-15, Philippians 4;6-7. If you are childless and you want children, please read the following bible passages day and night: Luke 1:13-16, Exodus 23:25-26, and 1 Samuel 2:5. Isaiah 55:11-14 says, *"So shall My word be that goes forth from My mouth; It shall not return to Me void, but it shall accomplish what I please, and it shall prosper in the thing for which I sent it. For you shall go out with joy, and be led out with peace; The mountains and the hills shall break forth into singing before you, and all the trees of the field shall clap their hands. Instead of the thorn shall come up the cypress tree, and instead of the brier shall come up the myrtle tree; and it shall be to the LORD for a name, for an everlasting sign that shall not be cut off."*

## Holy Spirit

Without the holy spirit (God Wisdom), mankind will have zero communication with God. If you do not have the spirit of God in you, you are not a child of God. Another hard fact. There is nothing in between, either you are with the devil or with God!!! Human beings have no middle line. Because there is something beyond its wisdom.

"It is through the holy spirit that we as Christians, are deeply grounded and rooted in the things of God." As all the information from the kingdom of God flows through him to us. It is through holy spirit revelations to us that the true meaning of words of the bible can be understood. It is through the holy spirit that we become children of God. He is the Godhead (God the Father, God the Son, and God the holy spirit), representative here on earth. The Holy Spirit is known by various names, including the "Spirit of God, the "Spirit of truth, and finger of God." His roles among the Christians are to; "comfort, convict, advocate, guide, counsel and help children of God over their daily challenges the devil present to them."

# CHAPTER 13:

# THE SPIRIT AS A SENDING AERIAL TO GOD

◄──────⟩•⟨──────►

Listen very carefully; we must learn to fight back against the devil so he will not mess around with our future. We must not watch as our lives are being destroyed by the devil and sent to hell every day. Whether you like it or not we are in a spiritual battle, a spiritual war, a spiritual fight, a spiritual struggle against the devil. This battle never ends until we die. If we are on Satan's side, the Lord may deal with us to get us to repent to be on his side. If we are on the Lord's side, Satan tries to cause us to fall, so that we can miss God's salvation. Do not underestimate Satan and his powers of deception. His ability to put obstacles in our path is great. He deceives some that are going to hell into believing that there is no hell. He also deceives others that are going to hell into believing they are going to heaven through their good work. Please note no single person will go to heaven because of their work. Those that are saved, Satan often tries to deceive into thinking they are not going to heaven.

As a follower of Jesus Christ, you have been chosen to be a soldier in a war against Satan and his forces. It is a bitter conflict. Satan will do all he can to discredit you, to hinder you, to buffet you, to persecute you, to deceive you, to tempt you, to snare you, to oppress you, to provoke you, to bring sickness on you, to embarrass you, to make you ashamed, and to make you afraid. Satan will try to entangle you with lusts, pleasures, and the cares of this world. He may use the deceitfulness of riches against you. Satan can give you false dreams. He can try to cause you to develop pride, to become stubborn, to become rebellious, and to despise correction. Satan can be expected to send all types of forces against you to try to stop you. But the good news is that we have been given God's armour to fight and defeat all these Satanic works in our lives which are discussed in detail below.

## The Whole Armour of God

Please note that armour is something impenetrable. It was used by soldiers going into war to protect them against cruising missiles, projectiles and other weapons of war. St. Paul made these comparisons to assure us of our victory without being harmed at all by the wiles of the devil. ***"Stand therefore, having girded your waist with truth, having put on the breastplate of righteousness, and having shod your feet with the preparation of the gospel of peace; above all, taking the shield of faith with which you will be able to quench all the fiery darts of the wicked one. And take the helmet of salvation, and the sword of the Spirit, which is the word of God; praying always with all prayer and supplication in the Spirit, being watchful to this end with all perseverance and supplication for all the saints."***

## Belt of Truth

Truth is to govern the struggle we are in. Standing in Jesus must be based on truth. It must be based on being founded and built upon "the" rock (Jesus). Jesus is the word – Matthew 7:24,25; John 1:1,14. *"It is written, he that believeth not the son (or the word) shall not see life"* – **John 3:36.** *"He that believeth not God (the word) hath made him a liar"* – **1 John 5:10.** *"And ye have not his word abiding in you: for whom he hath sent, him ye believe not"* – John 5:38. Our Waist must be girt about with truth (or the belt of truth). Truth should reflect righteousness. It is written, "And righteousness shall be the girdle of his waist" -Isaiah 11:5. The sword, which represents God's word, (Ephesians 6:17), can be fastened to the belt, (2 Samuel 20:8), the word is fastened to truth. The world today is on the verge of rejecting absolute truth. In the higher institutions of learning today, you can find sayings such as; there is no right or wrong answer, no such thing as absolute truth, as what may be true for you is not true for others". Well, Jesus Christ of the bible is the absolute truth, and if you are a Christian outside there you must defend this truth. We are not alone as Jesus Christ put it clearly – '*I am the way, the truth, and the life. No one comes to the Father except through me."* John 14:6.

When you speak the truth, know that Jesus Christ is the master of all truth, and when you speak lies, know that Satan is the master of all lies. It is only when you know the true source of the truth, that the truth can set you free.

The world today continues to struggle to know what really is the truth. How to say the truth and how to maintain the truth. If I may ask you today, what is the truth according to you? I imagine your answers to be along these lines: Truth is what I believe to be real to me; the truth is what others in agreement with me say and believe to be true; the truth is facts-based principles supported by evidence over a matter, situation or thing. These definitions as to what the truth is, plus other answers you could give me, do make sense and have elements of reality in them as to what really is the truth. Yes, these definitions are partly correct, but they are not the true definition of what the truth is.

Interestingly as well, these definitions of what is the truth are also undermined or devalued by these sayings; What is true to you may not be true to me, and there is no such thing as a right or wrong answer (meaning there no true one collective definition of truth.) Sometimes people who would want to know what the truth really is begin to ponder and ask the question; What then is the truth? if it can be watered-down like this!!! I want you to know today that you are not alone. I was once in this state of confusion to define the truth. But today I have good news for you as to what is the true definition of the truth.

Here is the true definition of the truth. Truth is a "spiritual being" who stays in you and enables you to believe, speak and maintain the truth. Truth is a person. Truth is Jesus Christ. Jesus Christ said in the book of John 14:6, *"I am the truth"*. When Jesus Christ is in you the truth is in you. Truth is a strong weapon in your defence against the lies or deceptions directed at you by Satan. Truth becomes your standing ground against all lies when you know and believe that there is the holy spirit, Jesus Christ and God almighty. Truth also becomes your standing ground when you believe what the bible says about the origin of all things (both living and nonliving). With this in mind, you can liberate yourself from all the lies in the world today. If you are a Christian you must admit the fact that Jesus Christ is the truth and you will not be deceived or struggle to tell the truth and stand up for the truth. When you receive new information contradicting this fact then you must always dismiss it by referring to the bible as the source of your truth. Jesus Christ said in the book of John 17:17, **"Sanctify them by your truth. Your word (the bible) is the truth".** If the opportunity presents itself to you to compromise this fact, then you must avoid it. You must have this rule of thumb, if it is the truth, I will join it and defend it, but if it's a lie then I will get out of it. Truth must be the first line of your defence against the devil. Truth is to govern the struggle we are in. Standing in Jesus must be based on the truth. It must be based on being founded and built upon "the" rock (Jesus).

The alternative to the truth lies in another spiritual being. I also want you to know that lying is an act of a spiritual being. When this spiritual being is in you, he enables you to speak the lies, defend the lies and struggle to tell the truth because there is no truth in him according to Jesus Christ. This liar is Satan. He has been lying and he has lied from the beginning of creation according to the bible. As he did to Adam and Eve in the Garden of Eden, he will also do the same to you today by giving you twisted information, half-truth, and half-lie. Because he knows if he had to give you a complete lie you would discover it straight away and avoid it. For example, he will not tell you to go and kill a person, so he builds anger within you that turns into a rage that enables you to kill the person. The bible says when the devil speaks lies he speaks from his nature because he is the father of all lies (John 8:44). Lying is the main problem today in the world as people try to defend themselves from their mistakes through lies. I want you to know from today that lying is what Satan will use to keep you in bondage. Keep away from lies and you will be free.

Power of the new information: it is only when you know the true source of the truth, that you can be "set free." It is only when you do this, that you can know the truth and speak the truth in your daily life.

Without this, you will struggle to do the right thing in life.

Say the truth and the truth will set you free. Jesus Christ is the truth. Let him live in you and you will never struggle to say the truth. It is not a choice, it is a must-do if you are a Christian. When you come to Christ as a Christian, you must decrease as Christ increases in you (humble yourself as you die to yourself and Christ takes over). It is not a joke; you are either Christian or not a Christian at all. When Christ takes over your life, he must dominate what you think, speak and do. Without these, you are not a Christian. It sounds harsh but a reality if you want God to change your life for good. Things of the body such as; the lust of the flesh, lust of the eyes and the pride of life must all be crucified. For a simple reason; God resists the proud and self-centred people and they will never see him. Doing one's own will must decrease as doing God's will must increase. Being loyal and obedient to God's demands and requirements must increase. The love for oneself, including obeying people above God, must decrease as the love of God increases in your life. When Christ dominates your life, it must be seen in areas such as; reading and believing the bible as the true word of God, helping people in need, praying and fasting and leading a repentant lifestyle. If you have done all of these you will see the seven seals of God manifesting in you as namely: power, wealth, wisdom, strength, honour, glory and blessings. Christ is the truth, you had better believe this before it is too late.

## Breastplate of Righteousness

The breastplate is part of our armour. The breastplate protects our vital organs in the chest area such as the heart and lungs. That armour or breastplate must be of righteousness. It is written, **"He put** *on righteousness as a breastplate"* -Isaiah 59:17 and putting on the breastplate of faith and love – 1 Thessalonians 5:8. Note, "faith and love." Love is the fulfilling of the law, thus, righteousness. The righteousness here is denoting the righteousness of Christ coming forth in the believer's life. The fruits we should bring forth are those of the spirit of God. Our integrity, character, and conduct should reflect Jesus. We should walk worthy of the calling we have received- Ephesians 4:1. Our righteousness is of Jesus. We must overcome evil with good. We must do what is right always in the presence or in the absence of others. The breastplate protects us from the toxic punctures of the satanic lies. The unrighteousness will lead to quick downfall and defeat by Satan as it is his strength. "None of us is righteous before God". If it was because of our righteousness none of us would have been saved by God.

The breastplate of righteousness is the strong weapon of your spiritual warfare against the devil. Righteousness is the perfect holiness of Jesus Christ. It means one who is right. And no one could be right apart from God, given his character of; omnipresence and omniscience. When you are in Christ know that you are standing not on your righteousness but the righteousness of Jesus Christ who died on the cross on your behalf for your sins. When you put on the breastplate of righteousness you must know that you are standing on the holiness of God who has redeemed you through the blood of his son on the cross having wiped out all the handwritings of requirements against you from the devil who had the power of death over you. Only Jesus Christ lived an obedient, perfect and sinless life on earth to give us righteousness in our standing with God. When God sees us, he sees the righteousness of his son through us, not our sins. We are completely justified by the righteousness of Christ. So, the devil has no right over you to kill you through disease, war, natural disasters, starvation and plagues. It also means that the devil has no right over your children, job, finances and your ministry. Practically it means that you may have committed sins in the past and the devil continues to remind you about it that you are not good enough to be a Christian. And your response to these accusations should be yes, I am not good enough to be a Christian and I do acknowledge that, but Christ died for me and I am standing on his righteousness for my salvation. You should know that you are elected by God and no one should bring charges against you as a Christian.

Having said that we must also be careful even when we stand on the righteousness of Christ, we must not continue to walk in sin. What we must know is that walking in Christ does not mean that we are immune from sin. But God wants us not to sin wilfully. So, what he wants is that when we sin, we must be sincere by admitting and repenting of it never to repeat it. Walking in light does not mean sinless perfection but continuous repentance in agreement with God by confessing our sins to God and not hiding them from him as he already knows them anyway. The fact that he knows your sins before you even commit them shows that you cannot hide them from him. He just wants you to admit that he is aware of them because he is the master of your heart. So, you must be honest with him when you have sinned. It is also by doing so that the devil must not bring charges against you in the court of heaven, to block your blessings. To remind you God will do nothing until you have admitted your sins; that is when he can rebuke the devil. Covering up sins means that you are still in darkness and the light of God is not in you.

We are not able to produce our righteousness because we are born into sin. In the garden of Eden, we know that our great grandfather Adam sinned against God and all humans are born into the sins of Adam. None of us is righteous before God that is why he had sent his son who came and died for us to regain our righteousness with him. Our attempt to produce or work our righteousness before him is disgusting to him. Even when we think that we have not committed any sin against God, our purest motives must glorify Jesus Christ as our saviour or else we will risk that our self-gratification becomes sinful and self-righteous. Anything mankind judges as good is abominable to God according to the prophet Isaiah. Because all of us have sinned and have fallen short of God's glory. We are never perfect on our own and we shall never be perfect on our own unless we put on Christ.

**1 John 1:6-8 says,** *"If we confess our sins, he is faithful and righteous to forgive us our sins and to cleanse us from all unrighteousness".* This verse indicates that God will only forgive you if you acknowledge your sins before him. He will only cleanse you of all unrighteousness if you admit that you have sinned against him and your fellow Christians. God hates sins and if you continue to commit sins you will never succeed against the devil if you deny it from God that you are a sinner. Confession of sins means that your success is guaranteed daily against the devil. You must have a blameless life in the presence of God when you admit and repent of your sins. The good news is that we cannot produce and work our righteousness as Christ has done it for us but we must repent of those sins we commit daily. The entire mission of Christ on earth was to reconcile God's people back to him by the blood of his cross. The purpose of the cross was for him to nail all our requirements on himself for the sake of mercy, love and kindness to give us salvation. All we need to do is to confess our sins daily and we will be right with God.

Being righteous does not only mean admitting your sins before God, but it also means that you must follow and do all the requirements the word of God demands from you. It also means following and respecting

God laws, statutes, commandments, and judgment. It means walking in his path and his ways. God wants us to pursue Christ's righteousness by imitating his character and conduct when he was here on earth. He wants us to turn away from our sinful nature and follow Christ's perfect ways. Our righteousness must begin in Christ and must be completed in Christ as God already perfected us through the righteousness of his son. We must be Christians who hear and do the word of God. If you hear the word and not do the word then you are not a Christian at all. You are just not different from those outside the Christian faith. Listen to me very carefully; your success is not in what you hear but in what you do. You must be a doer of the word not a hearer of the word. Righteousness means simply doing the right thing by God and others. Doing the right thing even when no one is watching; knows that God is watching you. That is the righteousness God wants from you. Righteousness is the living acceptable standard needed from us by God. We must shun all sins and stay away from them if we are to be friends with God.

## Shield of Faith

***"Without faith, we cannot please God."*** We are to take the shield of faith. What is faith? According to the bible; ***"Now faith is the substance of things hoped for, the evidence of things not seen."*** (Hebrews 11:1). In my own definition, faith is complete trust and dependence on God in all ways and for all things. It is an unwavering confidence in Jesus Christ.

The world walks by sight and believers (Christians) walk by faith. God is a spirit and we cannot see spirit with our own naked eyes. Although we are spirits as humans, we have a body that hinders our spiritual eyes from seeing spiritual things or other spirits. Hence, the spirits do see us but we don't see the spirits so long as we are in the body; it is only when we die and leave the body that our spirits will see other spirits including the spirit of God. The only way we can see spirits is through faith believing that spirits do exist including God, who is a spirit.

It is by faith believing that spirits do exist and they can communicate to us (mankind), that warrant the spirits to speak to us (mankind). The first spirit that will have encounters with us, if we believed and are baptised by it, is the Holy Spirit of God. It is this spirit (the Holy Spirit) that connects us to the other spirits as namely Jesus Christ and God almighty.

St. Paul referred to your faith in God as the shield of faith, because in war a shield protects important organs of the body such as the heart, kidneys, eyes and stomach. The shield can be used to protect other parts of the body depending on how the person uses it. Without faith, we cannot please God. We are to take the shield of faith. Faith is complete trust and dependence on God in all ways and for all things. It is an unwavering confidence in Jesus Christ. Faith in Jesus Christ (your shield) puts "Him" between you and the enemy. It is written, ***"The lord came saying, fear not, Abram: I am thy shield"*** -Genesis 15:1. ***"The lord, the shield of thy help"*** -Deuteronomy 33:29. The shield of victory – 2 Samuel 22:36 **NIV**. The shield of faith is faith in the lord. Through faith, all things can be overcome. Whatever the devil brings against you, believe that God is there, and he is willing to help you. Whether it is sickness, family problems, childlessness, depression, stress, or financial difficulty. Have unwavering faith in God at the weakest point of your life and you witness God move.

But we must also be careful with this as well because the bible says that ***"Faith without works is dead"***. Through your faith in God, you can qualify for his grace, which will mean you have your spirit living with him after you die. But God, upon creating you, had a purpose for you to carry out here on earth. This means that this work must be done by you before you go back to him. After you believed in Jesus Christ and you are saved, God reveals to you his assignment, where you work for God in what areas of this life he puts in you as your desires. Put in this context, Abraham our father of great faith was not justified by faith alone but his works also; he was asked by God to offer his son to God on the altar and he responded as God called. By doing this his faith was tested through his action (offering of his son), for God to see whether he was indeed willing and obedient to him. So, humans are not justified by faith alone but by their works also, and the only way you can do this is through your willingness to do some works for God. The reason why you were sent to earth by God was to come and work for him. You must be willing to do some work for God for instance; helping the poor, visiting the sick in the hospital, clothing the unclothed and visiting the inmates in prisons. Our Lord Jesus Christ said, when you have done these things to the vulnerable people then you have done it to him. Not only this we also have the responsibility to bring other non-believers to God if you are mature Christians, for them to be saved. God will be happy with you if you can recruit more people to his kingdom as he doesn't want any single person to perish. By doing these your faith is now becoming complete in God. ***"For as the body without the spirit is dead, so faith without works is dead also."*** (James 2:17-26)

## Helmet of Salvation

The helmet protects the head as an important part of our body. This helmet is of salvation. Multitudes of people sit in churches on Sunday, listening to the preachers, and are confident of their salvation. That there is life after death where you will sit with Christ on your throne just as he did. That Christ died for you to live this present life on earth abundantly. It is not a hidden fact that you can now know here on earth whether you are destined for heaven or hell. The way you live your life as Christians determines it. Nothing threatens the devil like a Christian who even if under difficulty knows that God is with them, and they are a winner.

When we are saved and have fully surrendered our lives to the Lord Jesus Christ, he will now reveal to us our assignments and guide us through them until we have achieved them. Once we are in God's perfect plan for our lives, we will find out that God had already decided and has a plan for us, the life we were to live on earth before we were born. To achieve this plan we are also given the holy spirit to help us through his power and authority which is within to overcome the obstacles placed on our way by Satan in forms of; temptations, sins we may fall into, and willingness and obedience to remains in our God-given calls or assignments. We were born as winners and victors because our God has won the battle for us and there is no need for us to live defeated, joyless and unproductive lives on earth.

## Sword of The Spirit, Which is The Word of God

The sword can be used for both defence and offence. With it, a person can block another weapon coming against them, but it can also be used to strike an opponent. We are to take the sword of the spirit. The spirit of God moves through holy men of God to speak God's word (2 Peter 1:21). As it is written, ***"Not by might, nor by power, but by my spirit, saith the lord"***-Zechariah 4:6. What is the sword of the spirit? Verse 17 concludes with-the word of God. Take God's word. ***"For the word of God is quick, and powerful, and sharper than any two-edged sword, piercing even to the dividing asunder of soul and spirit, and of the joints and marrow, and is a discerner of the thoughts and intents of the heart"*** (Hebrews 4:12). The word of God can cause Satan to flee. The word of God can make Satan tremble. You need to read the Bible, meditate in the Word, study the Word, and rightly divide the Word. We must take the word of God as medicine to remedy the situation we are in daily until there is a breakthrough (results): If you are sick, please read the following books day and night: Psalm 91, Mark 11:22-24, and Hebrews 9;14-15. If you are in financial difficulty, please read the following books day and night: Proverbs 3:9-10, Malachi 3:10-12, and 2 Corinthians 9;7-12. If you are in family problems, please read the following books day and night: Colossians 3:18-21, Isaiah 54:13-15, Philippians 4;6-7. If you are childless and you want children, please read the following books day and night: Luke 1:13-16, Exodus 23:25-26, and 1 Samuel 2:5.

The devil is scheming against you and me. Thus, you need to learn how to stand against his schemes, against principalities, against powers, against the rulers of the darkness of this world, against spiritual wickedness in high places. You need to learn how to extinguish the flaming arrows of the devil—those misleading thoughts, elevated emotions, and fleshly desires that burn inside you—prompting you to sin against God.

God has now given us the prescription for being strong, for standing, for wrestling or struggling, for withstanding the evil day against

Satan. The conclusion of these verses might be summed up in this: take and put on, be fitted with and have on the whole armour of God; this includes your waist being girt about, a breastplate, your feet shod, a shield, and a helmet. Take, put on, be fitted with, and have on truth, righteousness, the Gospel, faith, and salvation. Your strength is in the Lord, in the power of His might. Do everything possible to stand. And take God's Word, rightly share it, and use it as the Holy Spirit directs.

# CHAPTER 14:

## SPIRIT IF SAVED WILL GO BACK TO GOD

Our great grandfather, Adam had a body, soul and spirit. Adam's body was formed from the dust of the ground, soul (blood) which is the life of his body and spirit to communicate with God. Having said this there is no doubt of what happened on the day Adam and Eve violated God's instructions and ate from the tree of the knowledge of good and evil. God had warned them not to eat from the tree of knowledge of good and evil or they would surely die. We know that Adam's body and soul did not die on that day he ate from the tree of the knowledge of good and evil as his body and soul later disappeared after 930 years on earth. So, if the body and soul did not die on that day they ate from the knowledge of good and evil, then what else did die? We know Adam was a body, soul, and spirit. So, what died that day was a spirit. God, because of violations of his instructions he gave to Adam, withdrew his spirit from Adam. Adam had to live on for 930 years as a body and soul without spirit. Hence there was no longer communication between God and Adam as the result of violations of God's instructions. Adam was dead spiritually while still alive as he was not connected to God who would later on save his spirit when he had died. What happened to Adam still happens today to humans, as many people continue to reject God even as his spirit is restored to mankind.

Starting from Adam we now know mankind is tripartite made up of body, spirit and soul. Humans are spirit beings who have a soul which lives in the body. When a believer is saved their spirit is alive again in Christ. Jesus said in John 3:5 that we must be born again of the spirit. God (who is a spirit) communicates with us through our spirit. We have witnessed without a doubt that the body goes back to the ground when we are dead; whereas spirit and soul, either go to heaven if we are saved or to hell if we are condemned. It is important to note that spirit and soul according to the scriptures above do not die. They are immortal. The Holy Spirit who raised Jesus Christ from the dead, and who lives in you now, will raise you when you die and when you are saved. You had better seek the holy spirit now while in this life. God is immortal (deathless), by nature. God has also given us Christians the same immortality as those who believe in him. In His second coming, we believers who are saved will receive the immortal body that will be united with our spirit to live with Christ for one thousand (1000) years here on earth. Immortality is not the same as eternal life. Eternal life is received the moment a person trusts Christ, while immortality occurs at the resurrection of the body. The same will apply to the unbelievers; they will exist forever but in hell as spirits and souls, that are cut off from the life of God, and will not have immortality (body). When you are dead, the soul and spirit of the believer go immediately to be with God. As a believer, you will be alive and conscious in this state.

Though it is not your final reward as you await the second coming of the Lord Jesus Christ, it is a place of rest, waiting, activity, and holiness. This is how St Paul, who experienced it put it very well; that he heard inexpressible things that a person is not allowed to communicate. What a wonderful place to be. I am looking forward to it. What about you?

Regarding being born of the Spirit, the Bible shows us clearly the true Christian, that is, the person who is truly born again shall receive the gift of the Holy Spirit. The Holy Spirit shall actually dwell inside the born-again Christian. The evidence that the Holy Spirit is dwelling inside a person is by the fruits of the Spirit of God. The life of the person that has the indwelling of the Holy Spirit should reflect Christ, as they have the mind of Christ. A lack of the fruits of the Spirit, a lack of love for other born-again brethren, a lack of studying and obeying God's Word, and a lack of a Christ–centred attitude and speech are all good indications that even though a person may say they are born again and have the Spirit of God–they actually do not and are reprobate.

The Bible explains itself very clearly when we allow the holy spirit to do it for us. Let's make this observation; there cannot be a spirit of mankind without the spirit of God. In other words, if you allow the spirit of God to settle in you, then you have allowed God into you. It was because of the loss of the holy spirit, which was restored on the day of Pentecost, that you are now again a body, soul and spirit. But something must happen before you become spirit again – you must be born of it. John 3:6: ***"Jesus answered, "Most assuredly, I say to you unless one is born of water and the Spirit, he cannot enter the kingdom of God."*** This is a very tough condition one must meet if one is to be a spirit again. It is conditional upon believing in Jesus Christ who had restored us through his blood and flesh. So, having the spirit of God is conditional upon accepting Jesus Christ as your personal saviour.

Jesus Christ has set you free from the bondage of sin. Never let sin again rule in your mortal body. Whatever you are going through; sickness, depression, stress, anxiety, aloneness, discouragement, and disappointment let it not rule over you as it has no right over you. Everyday decree and declare the blood and name of Jesus Christ over your situation and it will be gone forever.

Sin came into the world through Adam, and sin was taken out of the world through Jesus Christ. The authority of the world was handed over to Satan by Adam in the Garden of Eden. Sorrowfully before Jesus came, mankind was drowned in the sin of Adam and people found themselves irreconcilable to God. God had terminated the relationship between himself and mankind in the Garden of Eden through the rebellion of Adam and Eve. Mankind became an enemy to God. It is to be noticed that mankind wilfully chose to work with Satan over God. This annoyed God to the brink for mankind to worship the creature rather than the creator. For the relationship to be restored, it requires blood. This, for example, was seen in the Old Testament where animal sacrifices were required to cleanse the Israelites of their sins. To that effect, no priest could approach the holy of holiest without blood on their hand or he would die. For life is in the blood for sins and for people to be forgiven by God, it requires the blood of animals. This did not please God as people continued to sin after their atonement. Indeed, the blood of animals slaughtered every year for people's sins became irrelevant and ineffective as cleansing agents for sins. And for this reason, God had to send his son in the form of a human being to live among us and die for us. With this God was pleased. Unlike the animals' blood offered as an atonement for sins every year, Jesus Christ's blood became the atonement for our sins once and for all. It is through the blood of the son of God that we as mankind became presentable to

God once again as holy and blameless. So, when you come before God as a Christian know that your sins have been forgiven whether small or big. God has done it for you.

Listen very carefully," Jesus Christ is the only way to God. He offered Himself as the only acceptable sacrifice to God on behalf of mankind – what a love. There is no salvation outside the name of Jesus Christ by which mankind will be saved. Controversial as it may be, but that is the reality many religions of the world such as Islam and Judaism and many more, must sit with or grapple with. This assertion was not made by any man but Jesus Christ himself when was here on earth. It is a fact many Christians should not shy away from but declare with boldness to the non-Christians so that they may be saved before it is too late. For there is one God and one mediator between God and mankind, the man Christ Jesus (1 Timothy 2:5). His mission here on earth was to save mankind who was enslaved by the devil. He was here to preach the message of the kingdom of God to the blind, deaf, lame and lowly in society. There was no pleasure at all for Jesus Christ to be crucified on the cross without resistance, as he was powerful and with powerful angels who could have wiped off the world in a minute. He had legions of angels, but he submitted to the cross without a fight. Think about that. Not only Jesus Christ but all of us as human beings are of God because of God's presence in us in the form of Spirit and soul. I wish people would get this message for their soul to be saved.

We now as mankind, after believing in Jesus Christ as the lord of our lives and his resurrection from death and receiving the gift of the holy spirit, are now body, soul and spirit. That is why St. Paul wrote in the book of 1 Thessalonians 5:23- ***"Now may the God of peace Himself sanctify you completely; and may your whole spirit, soul, and body be preserved blameless at the coming of our Lord Jesus Christ."*** This is what happened immediately when we were born again; we received the holy spirit, our dead spirits were regenerated and resurrected and will go to heaven immediately when we die. Just as our Lord Jesus Christ was resurrected (by the holy spirit), so too are our human spirits resurrected from death when we are believers in him. How beautiful is that to live forever and ever with God. This begs the question; are you willing to give your life to Jesus Christ today?

# BIBLIOGRAPHY

Anderson, Neil T. 2019. *The Bondage Breaker;Overcoming negative thoughts,irrational feelings and habitual sins.* Oregon: Harvest House Publishers.

Bradley, Michael. 2020. *Bible Knowledge.* 18 December. Accessed January 23, 2021. https://www.bible-knowledge.com.

Bray, Claudine. 2013. *Hope and Healings my True Story.* San Giovanni Teatino: Evangelista Media.

George, Malkmus, Peter, and Stowe Shockey. 2006. *The Hallelujah Diet;Experience the optimal health you were meant to have.* Shippensburg,PA: Destiny Image.

Hernandez, David Diga. 2016. *25 Truths about Demons and Spiritual Warefare.* Florida: Charisma House.

Hetland, Leif. 2017. *Giant Slayers.* Shippensburg,PA: Desting Image.

Johnson, Beni. 2015. *Healthy and Free.* Shippensburg: Destiny Image.

Leaf, Dr Caroline. 2016. *Think and Eat Yourself Smart.* Michigan: Baker Publishering Group.

McIntosh, Ron. 2017. *The missing ingredient:Discover the one thing that changes everything.* Santa Anna,CA: Trilogy Christian Publishing.

Munroe, Dr Myles. 2012. *Reclaiming God's Original Purpose for your Life.* Shipppensburg,PA: Destiny Image.

Stambaugh, James. 2000. *Blue Letter Bible.* 1 January. Accessed June 26, 2021. https://www.blueletterbible.org.

Tripp, Paul David. 2011. *Forever;Why You cannot Live without it.* Michigan: Zondervan.

Willard, Dallas. 2006. *Revolution of Character.* Hampshire: Ashford Colour Press.

Wommack, Andrew. 2021. *Citzenheaven.* 22 June. Accessed June 26, 2021. https://citizenheaven.wordpress.com.

# ABOUT THE AUTHOR

DAVID D.WEL is a Church Warden, Secretary, Administrator, Teacher, Author, and the host of DW Spiritual Care International Online Discussion Program. He is the author of two books: Fighting the Invisible Enemy; know the weapons of your spiritual warfare and Human Being as a Tripartite; Body, Soul and Spirt; understand why your body is a battleground between good and evil. He is passionate to bring hope to hopeless people through the word of God. For you to increase your productivity, he will help you unlock your potential within you by bringing resources, information, faith, knowledge, wisdom and understanding for you to live and enjoy the life you were born to live here on earth.

DAVID D. WEL, holds a master's degree of International Business and a master's degree of National Security and International Relations from Edith Cowan and Curtin universities in Perth, Australia.

www.ingramcontent.com/pod-product-compliance
Lightning Source LLC
Chambersburg PA
CBHW031246290426
44109CB00012B/451